THE PENGUIN CLASSICS
FOUNDER EDITOR (1944–64): E. V. RIEU

*Editors:*

*Robert Baldick (1964–72) Betty Radice C. A. Jones*

St Brendan was born in Kerry *c*. A.D. 484 and died at Annaghdown in 578. As a child he was placed under the care of St Ita whom he came to regard as his spiritual mother. He later attached himself to St Jarlath and in due course became a monk and a priest. In 558 he founded the monastery of Clonfert in Galway which continued to exist until the sixteenth century. The story of his second journey (565–573) became extremely popular and was translated into several languages.

Bede (Baeda) was probably born in A.D. 673. He himself tells us that when he reached the age of seven he was placed under the care of Abbot Benedict, but when the monastery of St Paul was established as a joint-foundation at Jarrow in 682, he seems to have been transferred to the care of its first abbot, Ceolfrid, and to have remained a monk there for the rest of his life. He has been described as the 'Father of English History' and wrote *A History of the English Church and People* (a Penguin Classic) and *Lives of the Abbots*. Bede died in 735.

Nothing much is known of the priest Eddius Stephanus except that he wrote *Life of Wilfrid* between 710 and 720 A.D. He appears to have gone on a journey to Rome with Wilfrid and returned with him to Ripon.

J. F. Webb was educated at Gateshead Grammar School and Cambridge, where he was sometime exhibitioner and foundation scholar of Queen's College. He was later priest of the Catholic Diocese of Menevia in Wales.

# Lives of the Saints

## THE VOYAGE OF ST BRENDAN
## BEDE: LIFE OF CUTHBERT
## EDDIUS STEPHANUS: LIFE OF WILFRID

*Translated with an introduction by*
*J. F. Webb*

PENGUIN BOOKS

Penguin Books Ltd, Harmondsworth, Middlesex, England
Penguin Books, 625 Madison Avenue, New York, New York 10022, U.S.A.
Penguin Books Australia Ltd, Ringwood, Victoria, Australia
Penguin Books Canada Ltd, 2801 John Street, Markham, Ontario, Canada L3R 1B4
Penguin Books (N.Z.) Ltd, 182–190 Wairau Road, Auckland 10, New Zealand

—

First published 1965
Reprinted 1970, 1973, 1981

—

Copyright © J. F. Webb, 1965

—

Made and printed in Great Britain
by Hazell Watson & Viney Ltd,
Aylesbury, Bucks
Set in Linotype Granjon

# CONTENTS

*To Francis J. Oxberry,*
*thinker, scholar, friend*

# Introduction

# HISTORICAL BACKGROUND

BEDE's *Life of Cuthbert* and Eddius's *Life of Wilfrid* are, next to the *Ecclesiastical History*, two of our main sources for the early history of the Church in Britain. Cuthbert lived from 634 till 687; Wilfrid was born the same year as Cuthbert and died in 709. The seventh century, in which they both lived, was a period of outstanding importance in ecclesiastical affairs, for it saw the conversion to Christianity of the Germanic invaders, the growing conflict between Augustine's mission and the native Celtic Church, and the gradual triumph of the Roman order.

*The Voyage of St Brendan* is set in sixth-century Ireland and provides a background to the later struggles in England by giving a glimpse of Celtic monasticism on its own ground before it was challenged by Rome. Behind the twilight atmosphere of myth and fantasy in Brendan's whimsical travelogue lies the character of a saint whose zeal as a monastic founder earned him the title of 'apostle of Ireland'. The *Life of Cuthbert* gives a detailed description of the daily life and missionary activities of that same Celtic monasticism after it had been brought by Aidan from Iona to Lindisfarne, where it later adopted the prescriptions of the Synod of Whitby. Cuthbert is one of the most attractive figures of the Lindisfarne school. His simplicity – a combination of personal charm, fervent piety, and alarming ascetical rigour – still captivates the imagination.

Eddius's *Life of Wilfrid* breathes a vastly different spirit. In it we see Wilfrid bringing in the Roman order at Whitby in 664 and putting the decisions of the synod into execution in the North almost single-handed. He has none of Brendan's quaintness, none of Cuthbert's charm; he commands admiration but rarely inspires affection. Some idea of the difference in spirit and outlook between the Celtic and the Roman

Churches can be gained by contrasting the characters of the
exiles of the Atlantic isle and the haughty, magnificent Bene-
dictine prelate. Yet in Bede and Cuthbert the two influences
meet. Despite his reverence for the dying tradition of Lindisfarne spirituality and his love for Aidan, Cuthbert, and
Chad, whose virtues and piety live on in him, Bede is a
staunch upholder of the authority of Rome, a zealous pro-
tagonist of the Holy See in all questions of law and discipline.
Again, though the organization and devotional life of Lindisfarne were Celtic in spirit, the community conformed to
the Synod of Whitby and Cuthbert on his death-bed exhorted
his monks to avoid as heretics all who celebrated Easter at
the wrong time.

The history of the Church in the North is well known
from Bede and requires only the briefest note here. Long
before Augustine landed in 597 there had been a flourishing
Christian body in Britain in contact with the Church on the
continent and sufficiently 'advanced' to have become a hot-
bed of Pelagianism in the fifth century. This community had
retreated into the West and North-West before the Teutonic
invaders, and made no attempt to convert them. Twenty-
eight years after Augustine's landing Paulinus travelled north
with Aethilburga of Kent when she became Edwin of
Northumbria's queen and, after the famous parley with
Edwin and the pagan priest Coifi, baptized great numbers
in the River Glen and established his see at York in 627.
Edwin was slain by Cadwallon at Heathfield in 633 and the
following year Oswald reversed the defeat by killing Cadwallon at Heavenfield. Oswald then sent not to Canterbury
but to Iona for missionaries to restore the faith. His brother
Oswiu, who succeeded him, was also Celtic in allegiance, but
Oswiu's son, Alhfrith, a pupil and convert of Wilfrid's, steadfastly supported the Roman party at Whitby.

Relations between the mission from Rome and the Church
of Ireland, Scotland, Wales, and Northumbria were far from
amicable. The Celts were extremely reluctant to give up their
own peculiar rites and customs when ordered by Rome to
come into line with the rest of Western Christendom, for they
feared that submission to Canterbury and York might lead

to political domination by the hated Anglo-Saxons. Let us see how the Celts came to develop differently from the rest of Latin Christianity.

The changing conditions in the Church in Gaul during the fourth and fifth centuries provide a parallel to the changes in the British Isles during the fifth and sixth, for the two bodies were both affected by the same movement – the monasticism of the Desert Fathers. The organization of the Gallic Church of the fourth century was based on the orderly system of Roman civil administration: bishops had their sees in important provincial centres; ecclesiastical law and administration took as their models the imperial legal code and civil-service procedure. The culture and mentality of the Church in Gaul was thoroughly Roman. Into this order burst the flame of monasticism – austere, passionate, democratic. Its mysticism came from the pagan East, had been christianized by the scholars of the Greek Church, and flowered into the severe ascetical ideals of the Desert Fathers of Egypt and Mesopotamia whose way of life John Cassian of Marseilles describes in his *Institutes* and *Conferences*. At first monasticism was suspect in Gaul simply because of its novelty; the call for extreme self-denial, voluntary poverty, and withdrawal to the cloister appeared to be a dangerous alternative to the settled decorum of life in the world, and the monks seemed to constitute a threat to the hitherto unquestioned authority of the established order. The democratic elective system of monastic government gravely endangered the traditional machinery of ecclesiastical preferment, especially as monks were sometimes elected to vacant sees. The dispute whether bishops should be recruited from the regular as well as the secular clergy was conducted with increasing acrimony throughout the fifth century. The popes sided with the old order. Celestine, in his letter *'Cuperemus Quidem'* of 428 to the bishops of Narbonne and Vienne, does not conceal his dislike of consecrating monks to the episcopacy and inveighs against the practice of appointing outsiders (*'peregrini et extranei'*) over the head of the local clergy: 'Strangers and wanderers, men who have hitherto gone unrecognized in the diocese, are not to be put in command of clergy who are veterans in their own churches, for thereby you will exclude from office men who enjoy the well-earned respect of their own people. Let there be no change at all in the college of candidates for the episcopal bench.' It is interesting to note that Wilfrid, monk and abbot himself, uses the same argument two hundred years later (Eddius, Chapter 30) in his complaint to Pope Agatho against the consecration of Bosa, Eata, and Eadhaeth. Celestine's decree seems to have had little effect on episcopal appointments.

The fourth-century British Church, like its Gallic counterpart, was episcopal and diocesan in organization. The clerics who represented it at Constantine's Conference at Arles in 314 and at the Council of Rimini in 359 were diocesan bishops. The spread of Pelagianism on both sides of the Channel and Germanus of Auxerre's first crossing to England to quell the heresy in 429 show that Britain and Gaul were in contact with each other. About this time Palladius the Deacon was consecrated and sent to Ireland as first bishop to 'those who believed in Christ'. Patrick followed him in 431. It is tempting to regard the missions of Germanus, Palladius, and Patrick as parts of a campaign to keep the Western Isles within the bounds of orthodox doctrine and traditional framework of government. Whether this is true or not, the Christianity spread by Patrick was episcopal in character. He was by no means Celtic and his writings do not even mention monasticism. The style of these writings, the *Confessio* and the letter to Strathclyde, betray a Roman provincial education – classical, if only rudimentarily so. The *confessio*, or *apologia pro vita sua*, is a continental literary form: many of the tropes and linguistic conventions in Patrick's book can be found in contemporary continental works, and his Chapter IV has detailed borrowings from Gallic theological treatises. From the *Confessio* and letter one can deduce the existence in fifth-century Britain and Ireland of an ecclesiastical set-up similar to that on the mainland of Europe. Patrick's home background confirms this view: he was born into an established clerical family; his father was a deacon and his grandfather a presbyter, just like the continental married clergy of the day.

By the sixth century all was changed – the monasticism that threatened Gaul had conquered Ireland. Having once found a foothold, the new movement was welcomed and spread rapidly in a country where it had only to accommodate itself to an hereditary land system of small rural kingdoms. Ireland had never known Roman domination, and consequently lacked the framework of imperial government on which the Church had been able to model herself in Gaul. The monastery proved a more convenient centre than the diocesan *curia* for dealing with a shifting and entirely rural population.

What were the features of the Celtic Church that made it so obnoxious to the supporters of Rome? Not doctrinal unorthodoxy. There is no mention of dogma or theology in their quarrels, because the Celts were as much part of the Catholic Church as anyone else. The term 'Celtic Church' is misleading because it suggests a separate denomination in the post-Reformation sense; in fact the Celts were completely Catholic in their views on the papacy, as the letters of St Columbanus witness. In the papal briefs in Book I of the *Ecclesiastical History* the Celtic leaders are addressed, and spoken of, not as heretics but as the pope's own subjects. Their tardiness or refusal to conform to disciplinary decrees did not amount to heresy or schism; their differences were ritual and administrative, and had arisen because geographical remoteness favoured the lingering on of practices elsewhere superseded, and encouraged the growth of local customs. Their main deviations were in the observance of Easter and in the function of the bishop.

The Easter Question is not the most enthralling of subjects, yet it inspired, directly or indirectly, most of the literature of the period during which the quarrel raged. What then was the controversy about?

The rules for calculating the date of Easter were four: it must fall during the Jewish month of Nisan; in the third week of that month – i.e. after the full moon; on a Sunday; and the Paschal full moon must not precede the vernal equinox. The dispute centred on two main points – how to calculate the third week of the month and how to reckon the date on which the fourteenth day of the moon would fall. According to the Celtic party the third week ran from the fourteenth to the twentieth while the Romans counted it from the fifteenth to the twenty-first: the Celts used an eighty-four-year cycle to calculate the fourteenth of Nisan, the Romans followed the Alexandrian cycle of nineteen years. Each side produced abundant and cogent arguments from mathematics and tradition to verify their claims; but the question was not one of historical fact or doctrine (Easter could be celebrated at either time without offending belief) but merely of discipline – that is, who had authority to fix the date. In the end Rome prevailed. Southern Ireland was the first area to submit. Bishop Cummian, Abbot of Dunnow, sarcastically sums up the attitude of Rome to the Celtic claims: 'So Rome is wrong, Alexandria is wrong, Jerusalem is wrong. Only the British and Irish know what is right.' Northumbria followed next at the Synod of Whitby in 664, and Northern Ireland at the Second Synod of Birr in 696. Iona held out till 720. Wales had remained aloof from the controversy throughout, but North Wales gave way in the late eighth century and South Wales later still. Devon and Cornwall did not submit until the tenth century when, after Athelstan's conquest of the West Country, Bishop Conan surrendered to Archbishop Wulfstan.

The bishop in the Celtic Church was not usually the ruler of the diocese. There was, in any case, no division of territory into clearly marked areas of jurisdiction, and therefore no real dioceses. The office of local ordinary was performed by the abbot. Sometimes the abbot himself was a bishop; but, more often, the office was given to one of the monks who, after consecration, remained subject to his abbot just like the rest of the community. It was his duty to perform, at the abbot's bidding, the rites and sacraments proper to his order. This strange variation from the normal hierarchy of jurisdiction did not imply any erroneous theory about the place of the bishop in the hierarchy of order. The Celtic Church held the orthodox teaching on the sacrament of Holy Order. Furthermore, there were variations in the baptism rite and the liturgy of the mass; bishops may have been consecrated by a single bishop without co-consecrators; there were minor differences in the form for consecrating churches and abbeys; and there are thought to have been certain ordination rites peculiar to Scotland and Northumbria.

The question of ordination raises a problem. Archbishop Theodore doubted the validity of Celtic ordinations. Chad's consecration was held to be invalid, and apparently he was reordained through all the grades of order even after three years' peaceful possession of the see of York. Theodore's *Penitential* seems to make reordination the norm: 'Those ordained by British or Scottish bishops ... are not united to the Church but must be "strengthened" again (*iterum ... confirmentur*) by the imposition of hands of a Catholic bishop.' The text may refer to a ceremony of reconciliation rather than to reordination, because the word *'confirmentur'* is ambiguous. The subject is full of difficulties, but even if Theodore did judge Celtic orders invalid, the Church has not ratified his decision. Such ordinations were and are considered as valid as Theodore's own. The charges of heresy and schism so frequently hurled at the Celts by Bede and Eddius were more rhetorical than theological; they were quite unfounded and never substantiated. The Celts were obstinate, even pigheaded, but the Roman party was not always notable for its tact and understanding in dealing with them.

In Ireland the monastic movement grew to such an extent that, although the monks never intended to supplant the existing organization, they soon became so numerous that by the sixth century the Celtic Church was almost entirely monastic. The period 480–680 is called the Age of the Saints because of the superabundance of holy monks. An eleventh-century chronicler, Marianus Scotus, makes this entry under the year 674: 'Hibernia, the island of the Irish, is full of holy men' (*sanctis viris plena habetur*). 'Saint' in this connexion means little more than 'monk'. The Age of the Saints was a time of intense intellectual activity: of study, writing, and transcription of secular as well as sacred works. Ireland became famous for her scholarship and attracted many foreign students, Alhfrith of Northumbria for example. The Age of the Saints produced a distinct ideal of sanctity, and its saints conform to type just as recognizably as the saints of the Apostolic Age or those of the Order of St Francis in its early years. The *Catalogus Sanctorum Hiberniae* classifies them under the Second Order of Saints, the monastic founders, as 'very holy', half way between the 'most holy' First Order of episcopal saints and the Third Order of merely 'holy' recluses. This arbitrary order of merit springs from the episcopal bias of the author of the *Catalogus*.

Independence and individualism were the keynotes of Celtic monastic life: each house was autonomous, most of them tracing their creation to some holy founder in the sixth century whose rule remained the sole authority for the community. There was no dependence of house on house, no Rule of St Benedict, no liturgical uniformity. Each monk might have his own spiritual director or *anmchara* – the word, translated 'soul-friend', sums up the personal intimacy of the relationship. Strict though the religious life was and based on unqualified obedience to the Rule, it yet left the fullest freedom for development of individual personality and talent, as the wonderful corpus of lyric poetry written by the hermits of the seventh century indicates. These anchorites, like the hermits of Egypt and Mesopotamia, had progressed to the life of solitude from the body of the community; they flourished in Ireland in great numbers and their way of life was regarded, by coenobites as well as themselves, as the highest possible way of perfection. When Cuthbert in his later years moved out from Lindisfarne to the lonely Farne, he was conforming to a long-established and wide-spread pattern.

One of the most interesting literary developments of the seventh and eighth centuries is the emergence of the saint's life in narrative form. In Ireland the plethora of saints in the sixth gave rise to a comparable output of biography in the seventh century. In England writing began later. The first English example, the anonymous *Life of Cuthbert*, was written about 699. Christian hagiography, of course, began with the first persecutions in the form of a martyrology consisting of a simple list of names and dates. The earliest kind of writing of any length is the sermon for the anniversary of the martyr's death; Hilary of Arles's sermon on St Honoratus is a fine example. This early form gave way to the *acta sanctorum* in which events were grouped under subject headings. Adamnan's *Life of St Columba* is a good example, with its division into three books – prophecies, miracles, visions – but as a literary form it was outdated even at the time of writing; for continental influence, in England's case the coming of Latin Christianity in 597, had provided new models. The most important of these were Evagrius's Latin version of Athanasius's *Life of St Antony* and Sulpicius Severus's *Life of St Martin of Tours*, itself modelled on Evagrius.

The narrative of the saint's life followed a set pattern: his marvellous infancy and vocation, the struggles and trials by which he proved himself a true athlete of Christ, an account of his gifts, miracles, and prophecies, the warning of approaching death, a farewell address to the disciples, and the death and miracles at the tomb. Bede's *Life of Cuthbert* follows this plan in outline and takes some details from Evagrius – Cuthbert's warnings against communion with those who celebrate Easter at the wrong time echo Antony's admonitions against dealing with the Arians. The anonymous *Life of Cuthbert* borrows much more freely from the *Life of St Antony*; the introductory chapters are little more than a collection of passages lifted verbatim from Evagrius, Sulpicius Severus, and Victorius of Aquitaine.

Muirchu's *Life of Patrick*, Cogitosus's *Life of Bridget*, and the *Life of St Samson of Dol* have a common phraseology probably derived from John Cassian, and the close verbal and stylistic similarities between many of the early *vitae* suggests the existence of writers' manuals of the types and models. Wholesale borrowing was not plagiarism but the mark of wide reading. According to the standard of the times, the *vitae* were learned works in which quotation and allusion played as important a part in composition as legend and tradition did in the provision of material. The borrowings and references in Bede's narrative *Martyrology*, for instance, show the author's acquaintance with more than fifty hagiographical texts.

# BRENDAN

Little is known about St Brendan and few of those facts are
undisputed. He was born in 484 or thereabouts in Kerry, the
son of Findlug and a descendant of Rudhraighe. He was
often known as Mocualti, from his great-grandfather's name
Alta. Domaingen, his brother, was bishop of Tuaim-Mus-
craighe and he himself made his sister Briga abbess of Anna-
down on the east side of Lough Corrig in Galway. At an
early age he was put in the care of Bishop Erc. The bishop
put him in the care of St Ita, whom the child came to regard
as his spiritual mother. On her advice he later attached himself to St Jarlath. In 558 he founded the monastery of Clonfert and the rule, dictated to him by an angel, was so highly
esteemed that it continued to be observed centuries after his
death. He went on two voyages to the *terra repromissionis
sanctorum*: the first and unsuccessful attempt took place
shortly after his ordination, and the second, the *Navigatio*,
lasted from 565 to 573. The Latin version of his voyage enjoyed enormous popularity and gave rise to prose and verse
translations in French, English, Saxon, Flemish, Welsh,
Breton, Irish, and Scottish Gaelic. Several of the incidents
are paralleled in Arabian folk tale (the landing on the whale
brings to mind the same occurrence in *Sindbad the Sailor*) and
Scandinavian mythology. The *imram* or story of an adven-
turous sea voyage, of which the *Navigatio* is a christianized
form, is common in early Irish literature. There are many
borrowings in Brendan from the *Imram Maelduin*.

Out of the amalgam of truth, legend, and literary borrowing, one fact is certain – that Brendan did in fact set out on
a journey. His reason for doing so introduces us to one of the
more picturesque ascetical practices of the Age of Saints, the
*peregrinatio* or voluntary exile.

Pilgrimage to the Holy Land, the tombs of the apostles,
and the shrines of the saints began as a popular movement
in the fourth century and spread throughout the West during

the fifth. The journeys undertaken were often hazardous and called for considerable endurance and sacrifice, as the opening chapters of Eddius reveal. Ireland devised its own form of pilgrimage, closely linked to the anchorite movement. The monk freely left his native land in order to release himself more completely from human ties and come closer to God in solitude. This voluntary exile was looked on as a battle in which the soldier of Christ went out to fight against the powers of darkness and to perfect himself through self-conquest. The heroic ideal of glory in battle is translated into Christian terms; the enemy is no longer visible like Beowulf's Grendel but is the flesh, the world, and the devil. The Anglo-Saxon poem *The Seafarer* marks this transition from pagan to Christian feeling – the glory which will survive the hero is spoken of in Christian terms: 'The best epitaph a man can gain is to have accomplished daring deeds of valour against the enmity of the fiends during his lifetime, so that when he is dead the children of men may praise him and his fame live on with the angels for ever and ever.' The exile left his country in order to find God in solitude, exchanging a natural for a supernatural home, a spiritual paradise in which the soul might be united to God.

Brendan set off with thirty-three companions, a rather unwieldy number; but voluntary exile, apparently, need not be undertaken alone. The entry in the *Anglo-Saxon Chronicle* for the year 891 mentions a group of three men who intended to satisfy their spiritual wanderlust together: 'And three Scots came to King Alfred from Ireland in a boat without oars. They had left home bent on serving God in a state of pilgrimage, they cared not where. Their boat was made of two and a half hides and contained enough provisions to last them seven days, and within a week they landed in Cornwall and shortly afterwards came to King Alfred. They were called Dubslane, Macbeth, and Maelinmun.'

The Old Irish *Life of St Columba* praises exile as an imitation of the life of Our Lord, the '*Verbum supernum prodiens*' who came down from Heaven to be a pilgrim on earth for our sake, and links it to the example of Abraham whom God commanded to leave home and kindred in Ur of the

Chaldees to journey to the Promised Land. The Promised Land is the type of Brendan's *terra repromissionis sanctorum*, which is set, in the sixth-century anchorite fashion, on an island sanctuary. St. Columba lists three kinds of pilgrim: he who leaves homeland in body only but not in soul (and therefore gains no merit); he who must content himself with leaving in spirit because circumstances prevent departure (a sort of pilgrimage by desire); and the true pilgrim who leaves both in body and in will.

St Brendan's Isle was long thought to have real geographical existence. Maps made before Columbus's voyage locate it near the mythical island of Antilla, and Columbus records in his diary that he had heard of its position. Sometimes it was confused with Madeira or the Canary Islands, and a document in which Portugal conceded rights in the Canaries to Castille called it the 'not yet discovered island'. Between 1526 and 1721 four expeditions of discovery set out from the Canaries, and the hope of finding it persisted until 1759, when it was realized that the belief was due to mirages.

Brendan is said to have visited Wales to study under St Gildas, to have stayed at Llancarven Abbey and to have founded a monastery at Ailech and a church in the territory called Heth, and to have gone to Brittany some time between his two voyages. True or false, these tales testify to the saint's popularity outside Ireland. Many churches were dedicated to him in Scotland, and a church at Brancepeth, in Bede's own county, bore his name.

The Latin *Navigatio Sancti Brendani* was probably written in the ninth century. Though later than the works of Bede and Eddius it represents a much more rudimentary form of hagiography.

# CUTHBERT

Cuthbert was born about 634 and died in 687. Bede's sources for the *Life of Cuthbert* are the anonymous *Life* by a monk of Lindisfarne, and the witnesses he mentions. The anonymous *Life* is so much a source that, judging by factual

content alone, Bede's work seems little more than an expan-
sion. He follows the same pattern of events and, out of the
forty miracles recorded, only eight are taken from other
sources. In style the book is a great improvement on its forerunner: the anonymous author wrote a plain, bald, rather
jerky account in threadbare language and scant detail; Bede
gives a continuous connected story written at a leisurely pace.
He fills in details of plot, uses fuller quotation, adds *obiter
dicta*, and smoothes out transitions from chapter to chapter.
From a collection of tales Bede weaves a continuous narrative. Take for example his working up of the incident in
Chapter 5, Book I, of the anonymous *Life* into Chapter 4 of
his own book. Here is the passage from the anonymous *Life*:

*Cuthbert sees the soul of a bishop borne heavenwards.*
On another occasion during his youth, while he was still living
in the world, he happened to be tending his master's flocks in the
hills above the River Leader with other shepherds. He was spending the night in vigil as was his practice and was praying unceasingly with great devotion and purity of faith when the Lord
granted him a vision. The heavens opened and he saw, not by a
drawing back of the elements but with the eyes of the spirit,
angels descending and ascending (just as the patriarch Jacob saw
them at Luz which was called Bethel) and the soul of a saint borne
heavenwards in their hands as though in a ball of fire. Cuthbert
at once awakened the shepherds and described the wonderful
sight to them just as he had seen it, and went on to prophesy that
it was the soul of a bishop or some other eminent person. He was
proved right, for a few days later they heard that news of our
holy Bishop Aidan's death had been spread abroad far and wide
at the same hour of night as Cuthbert had had the vision.

Bede dramatizes the incident by letting Cuthbert tell the
tale himself and, whereas the anonymous monk passes on
abruptly to the next event, he makes it an integral part of the
plot – it is because of this vision, because of the lesson learnt
from it, that Cuthbert decides to discipline himself in the
spiritual life. Similarly with the following story from Chapter
6, Book I, of the anonymous *Life*:

*The Lord sends him food by the wayside.*
There is one other miracle of his youth which I must not omit.

He was once travelling towards the Wear from the south. He crossed the river at Chester-le-Street and then turned off his route to find shelter from the rain and storm in some dwellings used only in spring and summer. But it was winter time and the dwellings were empty, so, weary and hungry though he was, there was no one to give him hospitality. He unsaddled his horse, took it into one of the huts and tied it to the wall to wait till the weather cleared. As he was praying, he noticed the horse raise its head to the roof and begin pulling down the thatch. Suddenly a piece of meat and a warm loaf fell out, carefully wrapped up in a linen cloth. When he finished praying he felt the bundle and realized it had been brought by the angel whom God often sent to help him out of difficulties. He thanked God, blessed the gift and ate it. Satisfied and replete with divine food he set off like Elijah 'in the strength of it', glorifying God.

In Chapter 5 of Bede this episode is linked up with the previous miracle, seen as a further step in Cuthbert's spiritual progress and used to illustrate Christ's words 'Seek ye first the kingdom of God and his righteousness; and all these things shall be added unto you'. Bede connects the two events by two short lines of introduction, makes them part of a developing plot, points a moral, and throws light on Cuthbert's character.

Plummer, in his introduction to the *Venerabilis Baedae Opera Historica*, criticizes the way Bede handles his sources. With special reference to the chapters quoted above, he says Bede 'shows a marked tendency to exaggerate the ascetic and miraculous elements, he amplifies the narrative with rhetorical matter which can only be called padding, inserts as facts explanations of his own, and has greatly spoiled one beautiful narrative'. A comparison of the two books, far from confirming Plummer's view, suggests that Bede was a much more competent writer than the Lindisfarne monk. The one 'greatly spoiled' narrative is Cuthbert's vision of the fall from a tree of Abbess Aelfflaed's shepherd. Here is the chapter in full from the anonymous *Life*; the reader can make his own comparison with Chapter 34 of Bede.

*How Cuthbert saw the soul of a brother, who had fallen from a tree, being carried up to Heaven.*

The most faithful Abbess Aelfflaed told me another miracle

involving our holy bishop's spiritual knowledge. One day when they were feasting together at Ovington, a place within his diocese, she noticed the man of God sitting at table stupefied as though in a trance. Without letting the others hear, she humbly asked him what was being revealed. He replied, 'I saw the soul of a servant of God, one of your community, being carried heavenwards in the arms of angels and placed among the choirs of saints, angels and martyrs.' She asked his name. 'You yourself will tell me tomorrow while I am celebrating mass.'

Aelfflaed sent a messenger to the monastery to ask who had recently died but he found them all alive. In the end, after careful inquiries, it was discovered that one of the brethren in the shepherds' huts had fallen from the top of a tree and had broken every bone in his body. The messenger returned next day and informed the abbess. She ran straight to the bishop who was busy dedicating a church, arrived breathless at the basilica at that point in the mass where the celebrant says 'Be mindful O Lord of Thy servants and handmaids ...' and called out the name, Hadwald. She realized that not only did Cuthbert have the spirit of prophecy, as evidenced in this case, but that he had the foresight of the apostles in all things, as instanced by the many accurate prophecies he gave of his own death.

Bede's qualities as a writer come through even in translation and persuade one to consider the *Life of Cuthbert* as a work of literature, simple and unpolished, but worthy to be considered on its merits as writing, not just as an 'interesting' historical relic. Bede's literary powers are more easily appreciated in a minor work like the *Life of Cuthbert* which was written as a deliberate rhetorical exercise, a stylistic improvement on the anonymous *Life*. The padding and emendations so displeasing to Plummer delighted the monks of Lindisfarne, for the book which they themselves commissioned, corrected, and approved could have had little other interest, since, factually, it has hardly anything to add to the product of their own monastery. It is Bede's one purely hagiographical work, not meant to be read in the same way as the *Lives of the Abbots* or the *Ecclesiastical History*. Much that Bede records is true; his main aim, however, was not historical accuracy but imaginative truth within the framework of a conventional literary form, the saint's life. This is borne out

by the miracles. Hardly any of them are original and most
are classifiable into stock categories: the Biblical miracle or
story which is obviously, sometimes admittedly, copied from
a Biblical model (e.g. the water from the rock in Chapter 35);
prophecies of the day of one's own death (Chapter 38); the
'competition miracle' (Chapter 41). These types abound
throughout the whole corpus of medieval hagiography. Some
of Bede's conform in detail to pattern – the vision of the
departing soul, for example, where, as in Cuthbert's visions
of Aidan, the deceased is always surrounded by bands of
angels and the visionary is always absent from the actual
death-bed. The Miracle in Chapter 29 is modelled on the
incident of Peter's mother-in-law in Luke 4, there is a similar
incident in Chapter 34, and the same miracle occurs in Book
V, Chapter 4, of the *Ecclesiastical History*. Both there and
in Chapter 29 of *Cuthbert*, the New Testament is referred to,
and in the latter instance actually quoted. The story has become part of the stock-in-trade of hagiography and is not
meant to be subjected to forensic scrutiny. The miracles taken
*en bloc* are a means of honouring and proving the honour of
the subject, a means of illustrating (and why not embroider-
ing ?) acknowledged holiness.

Bede recounts no miracle in his *Lives of the Abbots*, yet
his sources, the anonymous *Lives*, abound in wonders; in the
*Life of Cuthbert* the marvellous element from the anonymous
*Life* is heightened, and only in Cuthbert can one find examples of the fantastic bird and animal tales so dear to Irish
writers and still current in the Northumbria of Bede's child-
hood; furthermore, while several of Cuthbert's miracles are
repeated in the *Ecclesiastical History*, only one of Wilfrid's
is mentioned from the large stock available from Eddius, and
that, significantly, is connected with the priest Acca, later
Bishop of Hexham and Bede's devoted friend. Obviously
then, the miracles are primarily a literary device for expressing devotion and enhancing the reputation of the saint. The
unusually unthaumaturgic portrait of Wilfrid in the *Ecclesiastical History* is due to Bede's lack of enthusiasm – considering Wilfrid's attitude to Bede's favourites of the Celtic
school, this is not surprising.

One should beware of taking Bede too seriously in the preface to *Cuthbert* when he protests the trustworthiness of his material; he was writing, as he himself says with unconscious irony, *'iuxta morem'*. The references to miracles in his theological works bear out the view that in filling the *Life of Cuthbert* with wonders Bede was satisfying the demands of genre-writing rather than those of faith. In the *Commentary on the Gospel of St Mark* he writes, apropos of Chapter 16: 'Miracles were necessary in the early days of the Church. She was nourished with them in order that she might grow in faith. When we plant bushes we water them until they begin to stand firm, but once they have taken root the watering ceases. For this reason St Paul says the gift of tongues is a sign intended not for the faithful but for unbelievers.' This is a completely orthodox viewpoint, that, in fact, of the fathers of the Early Church who sought to stress the invisible miracles of grace within the soul rather than extraordinary visible wonders. Cuthbert's miracles are nearly always didactic, sometimes pointedly so, and illustrate the remark in Chapter 21 ('It is hardly strange that the rest of creation should obey the wishes and commands of a man who has dedicated himself with complete sincerity to the Lord's service'); but they are intended as much to adorn a tale as to point a moral. They record tradition and satisfy popular demand. The concluding words of the preface to the *Ecclesiastical History* provide an adequate criterion by which to judge the *Life of Cuthbert*: 'I earnestly beg the reader not to impute the fault to me should he find anything in the work that does not tally with the truth, for I have simply striven to follow the true law of historiography – that is I have taken care to set down for the instruction of posterity whatever I could glean from common report.'

# WILFRID

St Wilfrid was born in 634, entered Lindisfarne as a youth, left for Rome with Benedict Biscop in 653 and travelled with him as far as Lyons. He was introduced to Pope Eugenius by the Roman archdeacon, Boniface, returned to England in 658 and was given land at 'Stanforda'* by Alhfrith of Deira, to which Ripon was added three years later. After the Synod of Whitby and the expulsion of Colman he was elected bishop. Whether he became bishop of all Northumbria at once is disputed (Eddius differs from Bede on this point) but his election was certainly secured through Alhfrith's influence. He was consecrated in the Gallican rite at Compiègne but found on his return that Oswiu, because of his delay in arriving, had already given the see to Chad. He thereupon exiled himself to Ripon until Theodore reinstalled him in 669. By 678 his territory extended over the whole of Deira, Bernicia, and Lindsey. Ecgfrith, alarmed at Wilfrid's grandeur, moved that the diocese be split into four parts and secured Theodore's agreement. Wilfrid appealed to Rome against the decision, the first recorded instance of an appeal to the Holy See by an English prelate. On the journey out to Italy he made converts in Frisia. He won the appeal, returned, and was imprisoned and exiled by Ecgfrith. During this second exile he converted Selsey. In 686 he made peace with Theodore, and after Ecgfrith's death at Nechtansmere was received back by Aldfrith, returned to Hexham, and regained the see of York and the monastery at Ripon. In 691 Aldfrith and he quarrelled about land and he embarked on his third period of exile. The Synod of Ouestraefelda or Aetswinapathe (Austerfield), called in 703 to settle the dispute, ended in a deadlock, and off he went to Rome again. Aethilred of Mercia welcomed him on his return but he made no headway with Aldfrith. Finally, at a synod held by Archbishop Berhtwald in 706, Wilfrid and his fellow-bishops were reconciled and he received the monasteries of Hexham and Ripon. He died at Ripon in 709.

Wilfrid's achievement was considerable. He 'won' the Synod of Whitby and converted the North to Roman christianity. By his visits to the pope, his flourishing of Rome's

* This name has been variously identified as Stamford in Lincolnshire, Stamford Bridge near York, or Stainforth (either that near Doncaster or that near Giggleswick).

decisions before king and archbishop, and his zeal for the authority of the Apostolic See and her canon law, he put the decrees of Whitby into execution. This was no easy task, for he had many opponents to contend with – recalcitrant prelates supported and egged on by jealous princes like Aldfrith and Ecgfrith. In the end he won by sheer force of personality and, though it seems more a victory of principle than an actual gain (he started with three kingdoms and finished with only a couple of monasteries), the issues behind Wilfrid's seemingly petulant quarrels were far from trivial – the conflict of Church and State in the appointment of bishops and the erection of dioceses, the battle of canon law and conciliar decree against secular force, the clash of authority between Rome and the metropolitan archbishop or provincial synod. Wilfrid settled an investiture contest in miniature and established the rights of the Church as a body independent of the throne. The *Life of Wilfrid* is set against a background of high ecclesiastical affairs, the first steps in the growth of papal government in England. Wilfrid can justly be called the Thomas à Becket of the seventh century, and like Becket he rose to power as a royal favourite.

As well as providing details of the history of the Church in the North in one of its most crucial periods, Eddius gives a sidelight on the culture of the Golden Age of Northumbria – the period covering the lifetime of Bede, 673–735 – which produced (apart from the *Ecclesiastical History*, Eddius's *Life*, Bede's *Life of Cuthbert*, and the *Lives of the Abbots*) the *Life of Gregory* by an anonymous monk of Whitby, the anonymous *Life of Cuthbert*, the Lindisfarne Gospels, the Codex Amiatinus, the sculptured crosses of Bewcastle and Ruthwell, Acca's cross, and perhaps *Beowulf* too. Wilfrid is no minor character in the cultural life of his age. He brought back from the continent stocks of books, pictures, relics, plate, and silks; he erected at Ripon and Hexham buildings that were acclaimed as architectural miracles; he put glass into the windows at York before Benedict Biscop did at Monkwearmouth; he introduced the Rule of St Benedict in the North of England; and he reformed Church music. The list he gives of his own achievements in Chapter 47 is not exaggerated. Apart from his routine apostolic labours, he found time to convert the pagan isle of Selsey and to act as a precursor of Willibrord and Boniface in Frisia. This pioneer missionary work on the northern shores of the continent is often forgotten.

The *Life of Wilfrid* was written between 710 and 720 by the priest Stephanus, called, in an addition in a sixteenth-century hand to the Cottonian MS., 'Eddius Stephanus'. This ascription, though uncertain, has stuck. Eddius has been identified as the 'Aedde surnamed Stephen' in Book IV, Chapter 2, of the *Ecclesiastical History*, who is the same as the Aedde in Chapter 14 of the *Life of Wilfrid*. Whoever the author was he seems to have gone to Rome with Wilfrid (he uses the first person 'we' in Chapters 52 and 53) and to have returned with him to Ripon (in Chapter 17 he calls Ripon 'our church'). Whether this is so or not, he was obviously in personal contact with Wilfrid as well as with Acca and Tatberht, and was a passionate supporter of his master. His partiality sometimes goes to ridiculous lengths – one can hardly be expected to take seriously the claim that Aldfrith's death was due to his treatment of Wilfrid, the accusations of bribery against Archbishop Theodore, or the direct connexion between Ecgfrith's fortunes and his treatment of 'our holy bishop'. These and such-like pious prejudices in which the book abounds spring from Eddius's naïve bias – often engaging because the very naïveté allows one to read between the lines – but most of his facts are accurate and his silence on the events of the period 692–703, years for which he had no information, indicates that he was not devoid of historical conscience.

Considering his models, Eddius wrote a *tour de force*. Wilfrid comes through as a figure of almost Renaissance magnificence and temper, drawn with much greater realism than Bede's delightfully stylized picture of Cuthbert. There is no plaster-cast saint because the conventional mould has been broken. Traces of the pattern remain – infancy narratives, miracles after death, etc – but a new spirit has been infused into the old stock form, and the Celtic Twilight has given place to the clear light of ordinary day. The *Life of Wilfrid* is our first full-length historical biography.

\*

I have aimed at providing a plain, readable translation of three important texts. The *Life of Wilfrid*, one of the most interesting products of the Anglo-Saxon era, has not hitherto been available at a popular price. The translation of both it and the *Life of Cuthbert* are based on Colgrave's editions of the texts, while that of the *Voyage of St Brendan* is based on the recent edition by Carl Selmer – *University of Notre Dame Publications in Mediaeval Studies, Vol XVI (Navigatio Sancti Brendani Abbatis)*. This edition is the only critical edition of the Latin texts, and has not, I believe, been put into English before now.

I wish to record my sincere thanks to J. M. Cohen and Mark Cohen, to Dr E. V. Rieu, to the Rev. A. A. Craven, to Miss M. T. Mordue for her constant encouragement, and to Mrs Betty Radice for invaluable suggestions and guidance in preparing the typescript.

Gateshead, 1963                                    J.F.W.

# The Voyage of St Brendan

1 SAINT BRENDAN, the son of Findlug, great-grandson of Atla of the line of Eogen, was born in the marshy region of Munster. He led a very ascetical life, was renowned for his powers as a miracle worker, and was spiritual father to almost three thousand monks.

One evening, while he was engaged in spiritual warfare in the place known as Brendan's Meadow of Miracles,* a monk called Barinthus,† one of Brendan's own kinsmen, came to visit him. Brendan questioned him at length and, when the interrogation was over, Barinthus began to weep. He threw himself full-length on the ground, and remained there a long time in prayer until Brendan lifted him to his feet, kissed him, and said, 'Father, your visit ought to be filling us with joy, not sadness. Surely you came with the intention of cheering us up, so preach the word of God to us and then regale our spirits with an account of the wonders you have seen on your voyage over the sea.'

In answer to this request Barinthus started to tell them about an island he had visited :

'My son Mernoc, the steward of Christ's poor,' he began, 'fled from my sight in order to live the life of a hermit. He discovered an island called the Island of Delights, situated near a rocky mountain. A long while later I received news that there were many other monks with him on the island, and that God had worked numerous miracles through him. So I went to visit him myself.

'After a three days' journey I reached the island and found Mernoc and his brethren hurying down to the shore to meet me – the Lord had revealed to him that I was coming. As we went round the island monks poured from their cells like a swarm of

* 'Meadow of miracles' (*saltus virtutum*)='Cluain Ferta', Clonfert in Galway.

† Abbot of Drumcullen and spiritual confidant of Brendan.

bees to look at us. The cells were scattered far and wide over the island, but the monks lived in close spiritual union with each other, bound together in faith, hope, and charity; they all ate at the same table and always sang the Divine Office in common. Their diet was made up of apples, nuts, roots, green vegetables, and nothing else. At night, when compline was over, each monk had to go to his cell and remain there till cockcrow or until the rising bell was rung. My son Mernoc and I stayed awake to wander round the island during the night. He led me to the western shore where there was a small boat moored. "Father," he said, "let us embark and row away westwards to the isle which is called the Land of Promise of the Saints, that land which God will give to us and our successors on the last day." We boarded ship and sailed away.

'Clouds came down and covered us on all sides, so completely that we could scarcely make out the prow or stern of the vessel, but after we had sailed an hour or two a brilliant light shone round us and a country appeared before us, spacious, green, and exceedingly fruitful. The ship put in to land and we disembarked to make a tour of the island. We walked for fifteen days and still did not reach the farther shore. All the plants we saw were flowering plants and every tree was a fruit tree; the very stones beneath our feet were precious. On the fifteenth day we came to a river flowing from east to west. We stood and thought of all the marvels we had seen and wondered what direction we should take: we were eager to cross the river but were waiting for God to show us His will in the matter. Our ponderings were interrupted by the sudden appearance of a man surrounded by an aura of shining light. He greeted us by name and said: "Be of good cheer, brethren. The Lord has shown you this land which is intended for His saints. The river you see before you divides the island in two. You may not cross it; go back, therefore, the way you came." I asked him where he came from and what was his name. "Why do you ask me where I come from or what is my name?" he answered. "Why do you not rather question me about the island itself? From the very beginning of the world it has remained exactly as you see it now. Do you need any food, drink, or clothing? You have been here a whole year already without tasting food or drink. You have never felt the need for sleep, for it has been daylight all the time. Here there is no obscuring darkness but only perpetual day, the Lord Jesus Christ being Himself our light."

'We set out at once and the man accompanied us as far as our boat. He disappeared from sight when we boarded the vessel, and we sailed back through the same dense cloud as before and arrived at the Island of Delights. When the brethren caught sight of us they rejoiced greatly and expressed their sorrow over our prolonged absence. "Why, fathers," they complained, "did you leave your sheep to wander about in a wood without their shepherd to tend them? We are becoming accustomed to our abbot's leaving us quite frequently to go we know not where and to stay there for perhaps a week, a fortnight, or even a month." I tried to comfort them. "Brethren," I said, "please do not think ill of us. You are living before the gate of Paradise. Not far from here is that island which is called the Land of Promise of the Saints, where night never falls and day knows no ending. It is to this place that Mernoc, your abbot, so often goes. Have no fear, for an angel guards him on his journey. Can you not tell by the smell of our garments that we have been in Paradise?"

' "Father," they answered, "we know that you have been to God's Paradise over the sea, but exactly where it is we do not know. We have often been able to smell the fragrance issuing from our abbot's garments for forty days after his return."

'I had stayed with my son for two full weeks on the Island of Promise without eating a bite or drinking a mouthful, yet we felt so replete that anyone might well have thought we were full of new wine. After forty days on the Island of Delights I received the blessing of the abbot and his monks and left with my companions to return to my own cell – I shall arrive there tomorrow.'

St Brendan and his whole community prostrated themselves, glorifying God and saying 'The Lord is righteous in all his ways: and holy in all his works.' When they had finished praying, Brendan said: 'Let us take some refreshment and carry out the Lord's "new commandment".'* The following morning St Barinthus received the brethren's blessing and set off for his own cell.

2 St Brendan chose out fourteen monks from the community, shut himself up with them in an oratory, and addressed them thus: 'My most beloved co-warriors in spiritual conflict, I beg you to help me with your advice, for I am consumed with a desire so ardent that it casts every other thought and desire

* *John* 13, 34: 'A new commandment I give unto you: that you love one another as I have loved you.' This verse is sung at the Washing of Feet in the Maundy Thursday liturgy.

out of my heart. I have resolved, if it be God's will, to seek out that Land of Promise of the Saints which our father Barinthus described. What do you think of my plan? Have you any advice to offer?'

As soon as their father in God had made known his intention, they all replied, as with one voice: 'Father, your will is ours too. Have we not left our parents and set aside our earthly inheritance in order to put ourselves completely in your hands? We are prepared to come with you, no matter what the consequences may be. We seek to do one thing alone – the will of God.'

3 St Brendan and his companions observed a series of three-day fasts, to cover the period of forty days before they were due to set out. At the end of forty days, Brendan bade farewell to the body of his community, commended them to the prior's care (this prior later succeeded Brendan as abbot), and set out westwards with his group of fourteen monks to the island of a holy monk called Enda.* There they remained for three days and nights.

4 At the end of their stay Brendan received the blessing of Enda and of all his monks and set out to the most distant part of the region, where his parents lived. He did not wish to visit them, but, rather, pitched his tent on the top of a mountain that extended far out to sea, in the place that is called Brendan's seat.† Below, at the water's edge, there was room for only one boat to put in. Brendan and his companions made a coracle, using iron tools. The ribs and frame were of wood, as is the custom in those parts, and the covering was tanned ox-hide stretched over oak bark. They greased all the seams on the outer surface of the skin with fat and stored away spare skins inside the coracle, together with forty days' supplies, fat for waterproofing the skins, tools and utensils. A mast, a sail, and various pieces of equipment for steering were fitted into the vessel; then Brendan commanded his brethren in the name of the Father, Son, and Holy Spirit to go aboard.

5 As Brendan was standing alone on the shore blessing the harbour, three of his own monks, who left the monastery in

* Abbot of Ardmere and a friend of Brendan.
† St Brendan's Mountain in the Dingle Peninsula.

search of him, approached. They fell down in front of their abbot's feet. 'Father,' they begged, 'let us go with you. If you refuse we will remain here and die of hunger and thirst, for we are determined to go with you as pilgrims all the days of our life.' Seeing their plight he ordered them aboard: 'Your will be done, my sons, though I know what you have come for. One of you has done well and God will reward him with the place he deserves. The other two have a terrible judgement awaiting them.'

Then he stepped aboard, the sails were hoisted and they set off towards the summer solstice; the wind was fair and they needed to do no more than steady the sails. After fifteen days' sailing the wind fell and they rowed and rowed until their strength failed. 'Have no fear,' said Brendan, losing no time in encouraging the brethren, 'for God is our helper. He is our captain and guide and will steer us out of danger. Just leave the sails and let Him do as He will with His servants and their boat.' They ate every day about the time for vespers, and from time to time the wind would fill their sails, though they knew neither whence it came nor whither it was taking them.

6 Forty days passed and they found themselves without food. Then one day an island came in sight towards the south. It looked very high and rocky, and as they drew in to the shore they saw a bank, built high like a wall, and several streams gushing down from the crest of the island into the sea. They could find no harbour at which to put in. Being sorely tormented with hunger and thirst, some of the monks picked up their flasks to fill them from the streams. The saint reproved them for this: 'Stop, brethren! What a foolish thing to do! Since God does not intend to show us a way in just yet, why must you start assaulting the place? In three days' time Our Lord Jesus Christ will show us a harbour and a place in which to stay and refresh our weary bodies.' They circled round the island for three days and on the third, about the ninth hour, found a harbour just big enough for one ship. Brendan at once stood up and blessed it. On each side loomed a rock, cut away sheer like a wall and tremendously high. When they had all disembarked and were standing on dry

land, St Brendan forbade them to bring any gear out of the boat. While they were wandering along the shore, a dog ran towards them down a path and sat at Brendan's feet as though he were its master. 'You must admit,' said Brendan, 'that God has sent us a trustworthy messenger. Let us follow him.' He and his monks followed the dog till it led them to a group of buildings.

They entered and saw before them a vast hall, well furnished with seats and couches. Jugs of water had been put out for them to wash their feet. When they had sat down, St Brendan charged them: 'Be on your guard, brethren, lest Satan lead you into temptation. I can see him persuading one of those three brethren who followed us to commit an awful theft. Pray for his soul, for his body is given over to the power of the devil.' The walls of the room were hung with vases of various kinds of metal and bridles and drinking horns chased with silver.

Brendan told the monk who normally served their food to prepare supper. This monk found a table already laid, with cloths, rolls of extraordinarily white bread, and fishes. When everything was set out, Brendan blessed the food, praying thus: 'Let us praise the God of Heaven who gives every creature its food.' There was also plenty to drink. When the meal was over and they had finished the canonical hours for the day, the saint told them to sleep. 'Take your rest,' he said, 'for there is a good, well-covered bed here for each of you. You need rest; you are worn out with over-exertion.'

After they had fallen asleep, St Brendan witnessed the machinations of the evil one. He saw a little Ethiopian boy holding out a silver necklace and juggling with it in front of the monk. At once the saint arose and persevered in prayer till dawn. At daybreak they went briskly about their business of singing the divine office, so that they might be able to get down to their boat in good time. When they had finished singing, a table appeared before them, already laid for a meal, just as had happened on the previous day. For three days and nights God provided for His servants in this way.

7 Then they set out on their voyage with this warning from

Brendan: 'Take care, brethren, not to take anything with you from this island.'

'Far be it from us,' they rejoined, 'to mar our journey with theft.'

'What I forecast yesterday has now come to pass. That brother of ours is hiding a silver necklace in his bosom; a devil handed it to him last night.'

At this the monk flung the necklace from him, fell at Brendan's feet, and cried: 'Father, I have sinned. Pardon me and pray for me lest I perish.'

The rest of the monks cast themselves to the ground and begged the Lord to save their brother's soul. Brendan lifted the culprit to his feet and the rest of the monks stood up – to see a little Ethiopian boy pop out of the culprit's breast and cry out: 'Man of God, why are you expelling me from the home I have lived in these past seven years? You are casting me off from my inheritance.'

'In the name of Our Lord Jesus Christ,' Brendan replied, 'I forbid you to harm any man from now till the Day of Judgement.' Then, turning to the monk, 'You must receive the Body and Blood of the Lord, for your body and soul are soon to part company. You will be buried here, but that brother of yours who accompanied you out of the monastery will rest only in hell.'

The monk received Communion, his soul left his body and was borne heavenwards by angels of light, as the brethren stood looking on. Brendan buried him where he had died.

8 St Brendan and his monks reached the shore of the island where the boat was moored and, just as they were embarking, a young man arrived carrying a basket full of bread and a large jug of water. He greeted them, saying: 'Accept a blessing from the hand of your servant. You have a long journey ahead of you before you will find the fulfilment of your desires, but at least you will not lack food and water between now and Easter.' They received his blessing and sailed out into the open sea, where they refreshed themselves with food and drink every two days, while their barque was borne hither and thither over the face of the deep.

9 One day they sighted an island close at hand. A fair wind
sprang up after they had set course for it and saved them
from being overtaxed by the effort of rowing. On arrival, the
man of God ordered them all out, but was himself the last to
disembark. A tour of the island led to the discovery of
springs gushing forth to form vast streams teeming with fish.
'Let us sing the divine office here,' said Brendan, 'and offer
to God the spotless victim of the Cross, for today is Maundy
Thursday.' They stayed there till Holy Saturday.

In their walks round the island they came across several
flocks of sheep, all the same colour, white, and so enormous
that their great bulky forms quite blotted out the ground
from view. St Brendan called his brethren together and told
them: 'Take as many sheep as we shall need for the coming
feast.' They hurried away to carry out his order. One animal
was singled out and its horns were tied. One of the monks
took the cord attached to its horns and the sheep trotted along
behind him, like a domestic pet. On their return Brendan
repeated his command to one of the monks, saying: 'Take an
unspotted lamb from among the flock.' The monk hastily
did as he was bidden.

When all preparations had been made for the following
day, a man suddenly appeared before them, carrying a basket
full of bread baked in hot ashes, and other victuals. He put
these down in front of Brendan and fell down three times
full length on the ground at the saint's feet, crying out:
'What have I done, you pearl of God, to deserve the honour
of providing meat and drink for you by the sweat of my
brow during this holy season?' Brendan raised him up and
kissed him. 'My son,' he said, 'Our Lord Jesus Christ Himself has indicated the place in which we are to celebrate His
holy Resurrection.'

'Father,' the man replied, 'you will celebrate Holy Saturday here, but God has decided that you will celebrate the
Easter Vigil and tomorrow's masses on the island you can
now catch a glimpse of.' Then the man began to wait on the
servants of God and started collecting together whatever they
would need the next day. He packed these supplies and carried them down to the coracle, then said to Brendan: 'The

boat can hold no more, but in eight days' time I shall bring across to you everything you will need in the way of food and drink, sufficient to last you till Pentecost.'

'And how,' asked Brendan, 'do you know where we will be in eight days from now?'

'By tonight,' the man rejoined, 'you will be on that island you see close by and you will remain there till the sixth hour* tomorrow. Then you will sail westwards to another island, called the Paradise of Birds. There you will remain till the octave of Pentecost.'

St Brendan asked him how the sheep could possibly grow to so great a size – they were as big as bulls.

'There is nobody on the island to milk them, and since there is no winter to make them go thin they stay out at pasture and feed the whole year round. That is why they are bigger than sheep in your country.'

They blessed each other, then St Brendan and his monks set out for their boat and were soon rowing away.

10 Before reaching the neighbouring island, their vessel came to a standstill and the monks, on their master's advice, jumped into the shallows and fixed ropes to either side of the boat to enable them to drag it in to the shore. The island was rocky and bare, there was hardly a grain of sand on the beach and only an occasional tree here and there. The monks landed and passed the whole night in prayer in the open, but Brendan stayed on board. He knew perfectly well what kind of an island it was but refrained from telling the others, lest they should take fright.

When morning came, he told the monks who were priests each to say his own mass, and this they did. After Brendan had sung mass in the boat, the monks took out of the coracle joints of raw meat and fish which they had brought over with them from the other island, and sprinkled them with salt. Then they lighted a fire and put a cooking-pot on it. When they had built the fire up with sticks and the pot began to boil, the island started to heave like a wave. The monks ran towards the boat, imploring their abbot to protect them. He dragged them in one by one and they set off, leaving

* About noon.

behind all the things they had taken ashore. The island moved away across the sea, and when it had gone two miles and more the monks could still see their fire burning brightly. Brendan explained the situation: 'Brethren, does the island's behaviour surprise you?'

'Indeed it does! We are almost petrified with fright.'

'Have no fear, my sons. Last night God revealed to me the meaning of this wonder in a vision. It was no island that we landed on, but that animal which is the greatest of all creatures that swim in the sea. It is called Jasconius.*'

11 They rowed towards the island on which they had previously made a three days' stay. They climbed its summit, which faces westwards across the sea, and from there they espied another island close at hand. It was grassy, covered with flowers, full of glades, and separated from the island they were on by only a narrow strait. They sailed round it, looking for a harbour, and put in at the mouth of a stream on the southern shore. This stream was about as wide as the coracle. The monks disembarked, and Brendan instructed them to fix ropes to the sides of the coracle and pull it, with himself on board, as hard as they could, against the current. He was conveyed about a mile upstream to the source. 'Our Lord Jesus Christ,' he said, 'has led us to a place in which to stay and celebrate his Resurrection.' Then he added: 'I think that, even if we had brought no supplies at all, this spring would provide us with all the nourishment we need.'

Beyond the spring, on higher ground, there was an exceptionally tall tree growing, with a trunk of colossal girth. This tree was full of pure white birds; so thickly had they settled on it that there was hardly a branch, or even a leaf, to be seen. Brendan wondered why so vast a number of birds should have flocked together. So keenly did he long to unravel the mystery that he threw himself on his knees in tears and prayed silently: 'O God, to whom nothing is unknown and who can bring to light every hidden fact, you see how anxious I am. I beseech your infinite majesty to deign to make known to me, a sinner, this secret design of yours which I see before me. I presume to ask, not because of any

* A proper name, derived from the Irish '*iasc*' = 'fish'.

merit or dignity of my own, but solely on account of your boundless clemency.'

He sat down in the boat and one of the birds flew down from the tree towards him. The flapping of its wings sounded like a bell. It settled on the prow, spread out its wings as a sign of joy, and looked placidly at Brendan. He realized at once that God had paid heed to his prayer. 'If you are God's messenger,' he said to the bird, 'tell me where these birds come from and why they are gathered together.'

'We are fallen angels,' the bird replied, 'part of the host which was banished from Heaven through the sin of man's ancient foe. Our sin lay in approving the sin of Lucifer; when he and his band fell, we fell with them. Our God is faithful and just and, by His great justice, we were placed here. Thanks to His mercy, we suffer no torment: our only punishment is to have no part in the vision of His glory which those who stand before His throne in Heaven enjoy. Like the other messengers of God, we wander through the air, over the bowl of Heaven, and upon the earth, but on Sundays and holy days we take on this physical form and tarry here to sing the praises of our creator. You and your companions have completed one year of your journey; six more years remain. Every year you will celebrate Easter in the same place as you are going to spend it today, and at the end of your travels you will achieve your heart's desire – you will find the Land of Promise of the Saints.' With that the bird flew away from the prow of the boat and rejoined the flock.

When it was almost time for vespers, the birds all began to sing in unison: *'Thou, O God, art praised in Sion: and unto thee shall the vow be performed in Jerusalem ...'*, beating their wings against their sides, and they continued singing the verse antiphonally for a whole hour. To the man of God and his companions the rhythm of the melody combined with the sound of their beating wings seemed as sweet and moving as a plaintive song of lament.

'Let us eat something,' said Brendan to his monks, 'to keep up our bodily strength; our souls have already been fully nourished today with heavenly food.' After supper they sang the divine office and, when it was over, went to sleep till the third hour of the night. St Brendan stayed awake and called the brethren for lauds of Easter Sunday, himself intoning the 'O Lord, open thou my lips'. When he had finished praying, the entire flock of birds started to flap their wings and sing 'Praise him, all ye angels of his: praise him, all his host . . .'. They sang for an hour, just as they had done previously at vespers.

As dawn came up in splendour, the birds sang *'And may the splendour of the Lord come upon us . . .'* in the same measure and psalm tone as they had used at lauds. At terce they sang *'O sing praises unto our God; O sing praises, sing praises unto our king, sing ye praises with understanding . . .'*; at sext *'Let thy face, O Lord, shine forth upon us, and be thou merciful unto us . . .'*; at none *'Behold how good and joyful a thing it is, brethren, to dwell together in unity . . .'* – day and night they praised the Lord.

Brendan made sure that Paschaltide was a source of spiritual refreshment for the brethren, by having them celebrate the full eight days of the Easter octave. When the feast days came to an end, he said: 'Up to now we have used this spring, near which we are standing, only for washing our hands and feet; it is time for us to use it to replenish our supply of drinking water.' Hardly had he finished speaking when the man who had been with them for three days before Easter, and who had stocked them up with provisions for the feast, arrived with a boat full of food and drink. He unloaded the supplies and said: 'Men and brothers, you have here enough to last you till Pentecost. On no account drink water from that spring. It is too strong to drink. Let me tell you what its properties are: it flows from a spring and looks and tastes like ordinary water but, if anyone drinks it, he immediately falls fast asleep and remains in that condition for the next twenty-four hours.' Then he received Brendan's blessing and returned home.

The monks stayed where they were till the octave of Pentecost and were constantly regaled by the singing of the birds. On Whit Sunday, after Brendan had sung the community mass, their steward arrived with all they could require for celebrating the feast. 'You have still a long way to travel,' he told them, when they had all sat down at table. 'Fill your flasks with water from this other spring* and take with you loaves of dry bread which will keep till next year.' At the end of the meal he received a blessing and set off home.

After the octave day of the feast Brendan loaded the coracle with everything their steward had brought them, and had all the flasks filled with water running out from the spring. When all the gear had been carried down to the shore, the bird that had previously spoken to Brendan flew quickly towards them and perched on the prow. The man of God realized it had a message for them. It addressed them in a human voice: 'Next year you will celebrate Easter Sunday and the rest of the time up to the octave of Pentecost here with us, and you will celebrate Maundy Thursday in exactly the same place as you did this year. Easter Eve, too, you will spend in the same spot as this year, on the back of Jasconius. In eight months' time you will come across an island called the Island of the Community of St Ailbe. You will spend Christmas there.' The bird left as soon as it had finished speaking. The monks hoisted the sails and put out to sea, with the birds singing *'Hear us, O Lord, thou that art the hope of all the ends of the earth, and of them that remain in the broad sea . . .'.*

12 The saintly abbot and his monks spent three months sailing hither and thither across the wide expanse of the ocean, and all the while they had nothing to look at but the sea and the sky. They took food every two or three days. One day they sighted an island close at hand, but, when they were approaching the shore, a breeze blew them back out to sea away from the harbour. Round and round the island they sailed for four days without being able to find anywhere to land. The monks, with tears in their eyes, implored the Lord to come to their aid, for they had come to the end of their strength and were completely exhausted. After three days of fasting and unceasing prayer, they came upon a small inlet, so narrow that only one boat could enter. Near by there were

* The text is not clear whether there are two springs or whether the steward has changed his mind about the soporific spring.

two springs, one clear and one muddy. The brethren were hurrying off to fill their flasks when Brendan called after them : 'My sons, do not take anything that does not belong to you without permission from the elders who live on this island. They will be willing to let us have water, if only we ask. There is no need to take it by stealth.'

As they were all standing on the beach, looking round and trying to decide which direction to take, an extremely grave and dignified old man with white hair and a shining face came up to them and prostrated himself three times on the ground. The brethren helped him to his feet. He kissed each of them, was kissed by all in return, and then, taking Brendan's hand, led them to a monastery about a furlong away. At the monastery gates Brendan stopped and asked him who the abbot was and where the monks came from. Brendan repeated his question in several different ways but could elicit no response at all from the old man, except the gentlest movement of the hand indicating that the rule of silence ought to be kept.

As soon as Brendan realized that monastic silence was in force there, he instructed his monks to observe it. 'Keep guard over your tongues,' he said, 'or you will destroy the spirit of recollection of the monks here with your buffoonery.' The attention of the brethren was distracted from this admonition by the arrival of twelve monks who came in procession, bearing crosses and reliquaries, to give them formal welcome. They were singing as they came and greeted Brendan and his company with the following verse: 'Rise up you holy ones of God, from your abode, and set out on the way of truth. Hallow this place with your presence, bless the people, and vouchsafe to keep us, your servants, in peace.' When the verse had been sung, St Ailbe* the abbot came forward and kissed Brendan and the brethren in turn, then each of the monks in procession did the same. Everyone gave everyone else the kiss of peace, the guests were led inside, and prayers were recited as they went, as is customary in monasteries in the East. Then the abbot and community washed their guests' feet, singing the antiphon: *'A new commandment I give unto you . . .'*. After this the abbot preceded them into

_____
* Patron Saint of Munster.

46

the refectory in profound silence, a bell was rung, and they all washed their hands and were told to be seated. A second bell was rung, and one of the community rose from his place and laid out on the table roots and loaves of wonderfully white bread. The roots were incredibly tasty. The seating was so arranged that, all the way down the table, guests alternated with monks of the community. Loaves were shared one between two. Then a third bell went and the drink was served. With great amusement the abbot exhorted his guests to drink, saying: 'Now you can have your fill, with joy and fear of the Lord, of the water which, a short while ago, you wanted to take by stealth from the clear spring. That other spring, the muddy one, we use every day for washing our feet, because the water is always warm. Where the bread comes from or who brings it to our cellar are facts unknown to us. All we know is that God, in His kindness, sends it to us by one of his creatures. Every day we have twelve pieces of bread, cut from two large whole loaves; on Sundays and feast days God adds a roll for each of us, so that the pieces left over from dinner may be eaten for supper; and now, on your arrival, we have been given double rations. Christ has been used to feeding us in this way from the time of St Patrick and St Ailbe, our holy founder, to the present day. It is eighty years since this began and we never feel any older or more feeble. On this island we feel no need for cooked food, nor do we ever suffer from extremes of heat or cold. When it is time for mass or the night hours, the church lamps which, by divine ordinance, we brought with us from our own country, are always already lighted for us; they burn till daybreak and the flames never diminish.'

They drank three times, then the abbot rang the bell, and the monks rose from the table in a body and, with great solemnity and in complete silence, filed out into church, with St Brendan and the abbot at the end of the line. As they entered the church, St Brendan was surprised to see a group of twelve monks hastily genuflect and leave the building. 'Father abbot,' he said, 'why did they not eat with us?'

'Because you are here. The refectory table is not long enough to accommodate us all at once. They are going to

have their meal now; they will not go hungry. Let us sing
vespers now, so that the rest of the monks will be able to
come in and sing their vespers as soon as they have eaten.'

When the evening office was over, St Brendan looked
round the church to see how it was built. It was square and
had seven lamps inside – three hanging before the high altar
in the middle of the church and two each in front of two
other altars. The altars were square blocks of crystal and the
sacred vessels – patens, chalices, cruets – and other articles
used in divine worship were made of the same substance.
The twenty-four seats placed round the church were of
crystal too. The abbot's seat was flanked on either side by
a choir of monks. He would begin a line of chant, the choir
on one side would take it up, and then he would conclude it;
then the next line would be picked up by the choir on the
other side. No monk in either choir would presume to start
a line of singing: that was the abbot's privilege. Silence
reigned throughout the monastery – none of the community
would take it upon himself to speak or make any noise. If
anyone needed anything, he would go up to the abbot, kneel
down, and make a simple and sincere request for whatever
he required. The abbot at once would take his stylus and
write down on a tablet whatever God had revealed. This he
handed to the monk who had made the petition. Brendan
pondered over all this for a while, then said: 'Father abbot,
it is time to betake ourselves to refectory, so that we may eat
while it is still light.'\* They did so and the usual mealtime
order was followed.

The day's routine over, they all hastened to compline with
great alacrity. After the abbot had intoned the 'O Lord,
make haste to help us' and had sung the 'Glory be to the
Father . . .' in praise of the Holy Trinity, the monks inserted
the following: 'We have acted unrighteously and done evil.
Pardon us, O Lord, our merciful father. I will lay me down
in peace and take my rest; for it is thou, Lord, only, that
makest me dwell in safety.' Then they continued with the
rest of compline.

---

\* The *Rule of St Benedict* (Chapter 41) enjoins that meals should be
taken during daylight hours.

After finishing the day's office, each monk retired to his cell, taking with him one of the guests. Brendan and the abbot stayed behind in church to await the coming of the light. Brendan inquired about the way of life in the monastery and about the rule of silence, wondering whether it were not too severe for human nature to bear. With great respect and humility the abbot replied: 'Father, I testify before Christ that it is eighty years since we first came here and yet the only time we ever hear a human voice is in choir. There is never a sound heard from the twenty-four of us; sometimes the older brethren might express themselves with a glance or gesture, but only the older ones. And we have never known illness, either physical or mental, since we arrived.'

'May we have permission to stay here?' Brendan asked.

'No,' came the reply. 'That cannot be. It is not God's will. Why do you ask, father? Before you set out, did not God tell you what you had to do? You and your brethren must one day return to your own monastery. It is the will of God that you should be buried there. Of those two other monks, one will journey to the Isle of Anchorites, the other is doomed to everlasting death in hell.'

As they were speaking, a flaming arrow shot through the window and lighted all the sanctuary lamps. As soon as they were lit, the arrow shot back out the window, but the precious fire remained burning in the lamps. Brendan wanted to know who extinguished them in the morning. 'Come and examine the mystery for yourself,' replied the abbot. 'You see these candles burning in the lampstands – they never burn lower nor do their wicks leave any ash, because their light is spiritual.'

'But how,' Brendan protested, 'can material substance be on fire with spiritual light?'

'Have you not read of the bush on Mount Sinai, how it burned and was not consumed?'

They kept watch the whole night long, and when it was day, Brendan asked permission to set off on his journey.

'No father, not yet. You must first spend Christmas here with us and then stay on until the octave of the Epiphany.'

Brendan complied with the old man's request and stayed the required length of time in the monastery of twenty-four monks on the Island of the Community of St Ailbe.

13 At the end of the Epiphany festivities St Brendan and his followers were given a good supply of victuals and received the blessing of the whole community. They set off in their little boat with all possible speed and voyaged hither and thither, sometimes sailing and sometimes rowing, till the beginning of Lent.

Their supplies ran out, and three days later they caught sight of an island not far off. They immediately began to row hard towards it, for, by that time, the pangs of hunger and thirst had become severe. St Brendan blessed the place where they landed and they all disembarked. There before them was a sparkling spring set in the midst of a profusion of greenery. A rivulet led from the spring and it was full of every kind of fish pushing their way down to the sea. 'Brethren,' exclaimed the saint, 'what refreshment God has prepared for us after all our toil! Catch enough fish for supper, roast it, and pick salad and roots to go with it.' They did as he bade them. Then, as they were pouring out the water, he warned them: 'Be careful, brethren, not to drink too much of this water, in case it does you harm.' His words, unfortunately, were not interpreted with uniform strictness by every monk – some had one glass, some two, and some three. They all fell asleep – some for one day and night, some for two, and the rest for three. St Brendan prayed unceasingly, begging God to pardon what they had brought on themselves by their own ignorance.

When at last they were all awake again, their holy father addressed them: 'Come, my sons, let us flee, before worse befall us. This place is death to us. God provided us with food and drink, but you abused the gift and have done yourselves harm. Get in enough water, fish, and roots to last us till Maundy Thursday – calculate at one fish, one root, and one cupful of water per head each day. Then let us be off.' The sails were hoisted and the boat set off southwards laden with all the supplies St Brendan had ordered.

14 Three days later the wind dropped and the calm was so great that the sea looked as though it had curdled. 'Ship your

oars!' Brendan shouted. 'Unfurl the sails and let God steer us where He will.' And so they were carried back and forth for twenty days till God raised up a fair west wind for them. They hoisted the sails, at the same time manning the oars for greater speed. They ate every three days.

15 One day an island appeared in the far distance, like a cloud on the horizon. 'Do you recognize that island, my sons?' cried Brendan.

'No, not at all!'

'Well, I do. It is the island where we celebrated Maundy Thursday last year; that is where our good steward lives.'

Overcome with joy they started to row with all the strength they could muster. 'Do not be so foolish!' Brendan shouted. 'You will tire yourselves out. Is not the Lord our captain and helmsman? Then leave it to Him to direct us where He wills.'

Their steward ran down to meet them coming in and guided them to the place where they had disembarked the previous year. Praising God, he kissed their feet, beginning with St Brendan and going down in order to the lowliest monk, saying as he did so: 'God is wonderful in His saints; the God of Israel is he who will give power and strength to his people. Blessed be God.' Having unloaded the boat he erected a tent and got ready a bath for them – because it was Maundy Thursday – and dressed them all out in new clothes and waited on them during the sacred Easter triduum. Up till the Easter vigil the monks were occupied in celebrating the Passion.

Once the Holy Saturday ceremonies were over, mass had been offered, and they had received Holy Communion, the steward made the following suggestion: 'Board your vessel and depart to the place where you celebrated the holy night of Christ's Resurrection last year. You shall do so again this year and shall remain there until the sixth hour tomorrow. Afterwards you shall sail to the island called the Paradise of Birds, where you spent from Easter to the octave of Pentecost last year. Take with you all necessary food and drink. I shall pay you a visit next Sunday.' This they did. The steward stocked up the boat with as much bread and water, meat, and other delicacies as it could hold. St Brendan gave him a blessing and climbed aboard, and they sailed away.

They disembarked at the same place as before and there, in front of them on the ground, was a cooking-pot they had left behind a year ago. St Brendan stepped ashore, sang the *Hymn of the Three Children* * and warned his monks: 'My dear sons, watch and pray, lest you fall into temptation. Remember how God, without the slightest trouble, tamed, for our benefit, the fury of a monstrous beast.' The monks scattered themselves round the island and kept vigil until time for lauds. Later each priest offered mass. This brought them to the third hour of the day. Then St Brendan celebrated the sacred mysteries, offering to God the unspotted Lamb, His Son: 'A year ago,' he said, 'I kept the feast of the Lord's Resurrection here. I want to do the same now.' Then they journeyed on to the Island of Birds.

At their approach all the birds burst out in chorus: 'Salvation to Our God who sits upon the throne, and to the Lamb. The Lord is God and He hath shone upon us. Appoint a solemn day, with shady boughs, even to the corner of the altar.' Their cries resounded with loud flappings of wings for almost half an hour, until Brendan and his party, having disembarked and removed all their belongings from the boat, were finally settled into their tent.

When the Paschal feast was over, the steward arrived, as he had promised, on the first Sunday after Easter, bringing with him all the necessaries of life.

As soon as they had sat down to a meal, the bird who had spoken to them last year flew down and perched on the prow of the coracle, stretched out its wings, and made a noise like some great church organ. St Brendan surmised that it had a message to impart. It began: 'God has mapped out four places for you, one for each of the four seasons of the year, where you shall stay every successive year till your pilgrimage is at an end. Maundy Thursday you spend with your steward; the Easter vigil is passed on the back of the whale; you are here with us from Easter till the octave of Pentecost; and Christmas you spend with the Community of St Ailbe. After

* The *Benedicite*, from *Daniel*, Chapter 3.

seven years, not without great and diverse trials, you will find the Land of Promise of the Saints which you have sought so long. There you will stay for forty days and then God will take you back to the country of your birth.' The holy abbot and his monks flung themselves to the ground thanking and praising their Creator. When the venerable old man rose to his feet, the bird flew back to its place in the flock.

At the end of the meal the steward said: 'With God's help I shall return with provisions on the day of the Descent of the Holy Ghost on the Apostles.' St Brendan and all the monks gave him a blessing and he went off home. They remained till Pentecost, and when the festival was over Brendan ordered them to get the boat ready and fill their flasks with spring water. The coracle had already been drawn down to the sea when the steward arrived with a boat full of food. All this he transferred to Brendan's vessel, kissed all the brethren, and went back whence he had come.

16 Our venerable father and his companions put out to sea and sailed for forty days. Looking round one day they espied a creature of gigantic proportions writhing along in their wake. It was still far off but was charging towards them at top speed, ploughing up the surface of the water and shooting out spray from its nostrils. It looked as though it would devour them. 'Good Lord, deliver us!' they yelled. 'Do not let the beast consume us!' Brendan tried to console them: 'Do not be afraid, O you of little faith!' he cried. 'God has always looked after us and He is sure to save us from this monster and from all perils to come.' Great waves buffeted the boat, heralding the sea-monster's approach, and the monks' fear increased. St Brendan raised up his hands to Heaven and prayed: 'Lord, deliver your servants now, as of old you delivered David out of the hand of the giant, Goliath. Deliver us, O Lord, as you rescued Jonah from the belly of a great whale.' Just as Brendan had finished, another huge sea-monster lunged from the west towards their attacker and, spewing out fire, began to give battle. 'My sons,' cried out Brendan, 'look at the wonders of Almighty God. See how the creatures obey their Creator. The fight will soon be over and, far from its being harmful, you will be able to set down this event as one of

the glories of God.' The wretched animal that had assailed the servants of God was chopped into three parts before their very eyes; the victorious monster swam back the way it had come.

The following day they sighted an island, wide and well set with trees, and, when they drew in, the rear quarters of the dead monster were lying on the beach. 'Ha!' cried Brendan. 'That creature was going to eat you; now you are going to eat it. We shall remain here a good while, so drag the coracle high up the beach and look round in that wood yonder for a safe place for our tent.' He himself chose the spot to pitch the tent.

When they had put all the gear into the tent, Brendan told them to cut enough meat from the carcass to last them three months – 'For animals will come in the night and pick it clean.' They did as they were bidden and stored away as much meat as they would need. When this task, which kept them busy till vesper time, was completed, they asked, 'How, father, will we be able to survive here without water?'

'Do you imagine God finds it harder to provide water than food? Walk towards the southern shore. There you will find a sparkling spring and plentiful vegetation. Bring me some, but not too much.'

They found everything as he had said. Their stay on the island was lengthened to three months, because foul weather at sea – heavy rain and hail storms – kept them from putting out. The monks went to see if what Brendan had said would happen to the fish had in fact taken place. When they reached the spot where the carcass had been, they found nothing but bones. Back they came at once. 'Father,' they said, 'you were right about the beast.'

'I knew you would not be satisfied until you had seen for yourself. Here is another piece of information for you; a great lump of fish will be washed up tonight and will provide a meal for you tomorrow.' The next day the fish was lying on the beach, just as he had foretold. The monks took as much as they could carry. 'Preserve it carefully in salt,' said Brendan. 'You will need it later. God will give us fine weather today, tomorrow, and the day after tomorrow, and the sea will be calm. Then we shall leave.'

Three days later he ordered them to load the coracle, fill
their leather water-bottles and any other vessels, and to gather
shoots and green plants for his own use – for, since his ordination, Brendan had never eaten meat. Everything was loaded
on board, the sails were spread and they set off southwards.

17 One day they saw an island in the distance. 'Do you see that
island?' Brendan asked.

'Yes, we see it,' they replied.

'There are three groups of people living there: boys, young
men, and elders. One of our party will leave us to go and live
with them.'

The monks were eager to know who it was and persisted
in asking till, seeing how crestfallen they were, Brendan gave
in. 'That monk there,' he said, pointing to one of the three
who had left the monastery to follow him at the beginning of
the voyage.

The boat came close in to the shore. The island itself was
remarkably flat and low, and seemed to be literally at sea
level; it was completely bare of trees or of anything which
could act as a windshield. It was very wide and was covered
with purple and white *caltae**. Three bands of men could be
discerned, just as Brendan had said, and they were standing
apart from each other, the distance between them being
roughly as far as a stone could be cast by a sling. They moved
about continually except when one band stopped and sang
'The saints shall go from strength to strength, the God of
gods shall be seen in Sion.' When the group came to the end
of the verse, another band would take it up again, and so the
singing went on unceasingly. The first band, the boys, was
dressed in pure white garments, the second group in jacinth
apparel, and the third in purple dalmatics†.

Brendan's party landed about the fourth hour. At sext the
groups sang in unison '*God be merciful unto us ...*' – which
was sung right through to the end, '*Haste thee, O God, to
deliver me ...*' and, as a third psalm, '*I believed, and therefore will I speak ...*' and then a prayer. At none they sang
another three psalms: '*Out of the depths have I cried to thee,*

* The meaning of '*calta*' is uncertain. It is either a fruit or a flower.
† The colours symbolize respectively innocence, vigour, and maturity.

O Lord ...', 'Behold how good and joyful ...', and 'Praise the Lord, O Jerusalem ...'. The psalms for vespers were: 'Thou, O God, art praised in Sion ...', 'Praise the Lord, O my soul ...', 'O Lord, my God ...', 'Praise the Lord, ye servants ...' and then, one after another, the fifteen 'Songs of Degrees'.* These latter were sung sitting down.

An astoundingly white cloud came down over the island at the end of the singing and made everything invisible, such was the density of vapour; but the singing continued audibly till it was time for lauds. The psalms for lauds were: 'O praise the Lord of Heaven ...', 'O sing unto the Lord a new song ...', and 'O praise God in his holiness ...'. Then twelve psalms were sung, one after the other, as they occur in the psalter. The cloud lifted at daybreak and the three groups at once sang three psalms: 'Have mercy upon me, O God ...', 'O God, thou art my God; early will I seek thee ...', and 'Lord, thou hast been our refuge ...' At terce they sang another three: 'O clap your hands together, all ye people ...', 'Save me, O God, for thy name's sake ...', and 'I am well pleased ...' with the *Alleluia*. Then the divine victim was offered up and all received Communion, saying: 'Receive this sacred Body and Blood of your Lord and Saviour unto life everlasting.'†

Two boys came out at the end of mass, carrying a basket of purple *caltae*, which they put into the boat, saying: 'Take with you some of the produce of this island of steadfast men. Let your brother come with us, then set out in peace.' St Brendan called the monk who was about to leave them. 'Kiss your brethren,' he said, 'and go with those who are calling you, for you have been found worthy of a place in this wonderful fellowship. Blessed was the hour in which your mother bore you!' The monk kissed his abbot and fellow monks and Brendan bade him farewell: 'My son, remember all the many benefits God has given you in this world. Go in peace, and pray for us.' The monk followed the two youths to their group.

* *Psalms* 119–133 (Vulgate), 120–134 (A.V.).

† This verse, ascribed to St Sechnall, is said to be the oldest Latin Eucharistic hymn extant.

Our venerable father and his companions began to row away. At the ninth hour Brendan told them to restore their strength with *caltae* from the island of steadfast men. He picked out one himself and was astonished to find it so huge and full of juice. 'Never in my life,' he exclaimed, 'have I heard, or even read, of *caltae* of this size.' They were all the same size, large and globular in shape. He asked for a cup, and from one fruit alone squeezed out a quart of juice. This was shared among the twelve monks and for the next twelve days the party lived on one fruit each day. The *caltae* left a constant taste of honey in their mouths.

18 When the fruit had all been eaten, Brendan ordered a three-day fast. At the end of the third day an enormous bird flew straight towards the boat, carrying in its beak a branch of some unfamiliar tree. On the end of this branch hung a large bunch of bright red grapes. The bird dropped the branch into Brendan's lap. Calling together the monks he exhorted them to eat: 'Look at the meal God has sent us! Take and eat.' Each of the grapes was as big as an apple. Brendan shared the bunch out, grape by grape, and it lasted twelve days. After this they fasted again.

The island they came upon three days later was thickly set in every part with trees bearing the same kind of fruit as the bird had brought them. These trees were all the same colour and so full of fruit–it was incredible–that the branches were bowed down to the ground. No other species of tree was to be found and not one of the fruit trees was sterile. They put in to the shore. Brendan disembarked to beat the bounds of the place, and the monks stayed on board till he came back. The island exhaled a fragrant odour, like the smell of pomegranates pervading the rooms of a house. They were so much refreshed by the sweet smell wafting over them that the edge was quite taken off their fast. Meanwhile Brendan had discovered six springs set in the middle of a patch of lush ground which was thick with green plants and shoots. He came back with his arms full of the first fruits of the island's produce. 'Come ashore!' he shouted. 'Fix the tent and take your fill of these prime fruits of the land to which God has led us.' For forty days they fed well on grapes, salads, and shoots. Then

they left, taking with them as much as the boat could hold.
19 They hoisted sail and drove before the wind. As they were
sailing along, a bird appeared in the distance, flying towards
them. It was a gryphon. The brethren cried out to Brendan
in consternation, 'Help! That thing is coming to eat us.'

'Fear not,' Brendan replied. 'God has been our helper up
to now and will not fail us this time.'

The gryphon was stretching out its claws to catch the
monks when, suddenly, the bird that had brought the grapes
swooped rapidly down upon it. The gryphon tried to devour
it but the other defended itself and finally gained the upper
hand. It tore out the gryphon's eyes and the gryphon then
flew higher and higher, till it was almost lost from sight. The
other bird gave chase and killed it; the carcass fell into the
sea near the coracle. The victorious bird flew back to where it
had come from.

20 St Brendan and his mariners caught sight of the Island of the
Community of St Ailbe a few days later. Christmas was spent
there, and after the festivities were over Brendan's party received the blessing of the abbot and community and sailed
across the ocean for a long while. The only rest they had from
navigating was at Christmas and Easter, which they spent at
the usual places.

21 St Peter's Day was celebrated by St Brendan at sea, and the
water was so clear that the monks could see every movement
of life beneath the boat; so clear, indeed, that the animals on
the ocean bed seemed near enough to touch. If the monks
looked down into the deep, they could see many different
kinds of creatures lying on the sandy bottom like flocks at
pasture, so numerous that, lying head to tail, and moving
gently with the swell, they looked like a city on the march.

The monks urged their master to say mass silently lest the
fish, hearing his voice, might rise up and attack them. Brendan chaffed them: 'I am surprised at your foolishness. What—
are you afraid of these creatures? Have you not several times
landed on the monarch of the deep, the beast who eats all
other sea creatures? Why, you have sat down on his back and
sung psalms, have even gathered sticks, lighted a fire and
cooked food – and all this without showing fear. Then how

can you be afraid of these? Is not Our Lord Jesus Christ the Lord of Creation? Can he not make all creatures docile?' Brendan sang at the top of his voice, causing the brethren to cast an anxious eye in the direction of the fish, but at the sound of singing the fish rose up from the sea bed and swam round and round the coracle. There was nothing to be seen but crowds of swimming forms. They did not come close but, keeping their distance, swam back and forth till mass was over. Then they scurried away on their own tracks over the paths of the ocean, out of sight of the servants of God. St Brendan journeyed on, and after going at full sail for a week, with fair winds every day, still had not crossed the open sea.

22  One day, when the masses were over, they noticed a column rising out of the sea. It seemed quite near at hand but turned out to be a good three days' journey away. When they reached it, Brendan gazed upwards but could hardly see the top because of its great height: it was higher than the sky. This column was covered with a most unusual canopy – so strange indeed that the coracle could pass through the openings in it but no one could tell what substance it was made of. It was the colour of silver and seemed harder than marble. The column itself was of pure crystal.*

'Ship the oars!' Brendan commanded. 'Take down the sails and hold back the ribs of the canopy.' The canopy was so big that it extended a mile on either side of the column and went down into the sea. 'Now draw the boat through the opening,' Brendan continued, 'and let us inspect the wonders of God, our Maker.' They entered and gazed all round: the sea was as transparent as glass and everything in it was clearly visible; they could look at the foundations of the column below the surface and see the top of the canopy reflected in the water. The sun shone inside the canopy as brightly as on the open sea. Brendan measured four different apertures in the canopy and found them each four cubits long.

They spent a whole day in rowing along one side of the

---

*The sudden appearance of the column and canopy is bewildering and there is no explanation given in the text. The incident suggests a meeting with an iceberg. Details of shape and size seem to have been taken from *Ezekiel*, Chapters 40 and 41, or Chapter 21 of the *Apocalypse*.

canopy and could still feel the heat of the sun until the ninth hour, despite the shade cast by the canopy. The length of each side was one thousand four hundred cubits. Brendan measured a side of the towering canopy a day, and as there were four sides the task took four days to complete. A chalice, made of the same substance as the canopy, came to light in the southern reaches on the fourth day; with it, lying on a niche in the canopy, was a paten the same colour as the column. St Brendan immediately picked up the vessels. 'This miracle,' he said, 'is the work of Our Lord Jesus Christ. These two gifts have been given to me so that the story of our travels may be widely believed.' He ordered them to sing the Divine Office and then to take some food, because the sight of the column had cast out of their mind all thought of food and drink.

The following day they set off southwards. Some of the brethren held back the ribs of the canopy to let the others get the mast and sails ready for hoisting as soon as the boat would be clear of the opening. Once the mast and sails were hoisted they were caught by a good strong wind, which carried them north for eight days, so that all they had to do was keep an eye on the steerage and rigging.

23 The eighth day found them near a stony island quite without grass or trees. The countryside was wild and dotted with slag heaps and numerous forges. 'Brethren,' said Brendan, 'that island makes me feel uneasy. I have no desire to land nor even to go near, yet the wind is taking us straight towards it!' They had only gone forward about a stone's throw when the blowing of bellows and the clang of hammer on anvil dinned in their ears like thunder. Crossing himself with the sign of Christ's victory, he prayed: 'Lord Jesus Christ deliver us from this island.' Hardly had he finished the prayer when one of the inhabitants, a very swarthy, evil-looking man, with a bright red face, came out of a forge to perform some task or other. He caught sight of the coracle approaching and turned back. St Brendan crossed himself again. 'My sons,' he shouted, 'let us flee from this place. Up with the sails and row as fast as you can.' He had just finished the sentence when the savage rushed down to the beach carrying a huge piece of

blazing slag in a pair of tongs. This he hurled at the boat, but it shot over their heads and fell about a furlong beyond them. It struck the water and seethed like a live ember from a volcano. Smoke rose up from the sea as from a fiery furnace.

When the boat had sailed about a mile from where the slag fell, all the inhabitants of the island rushed down to the beach, each carrying a glowing mass of slag. Some aimed at the servants of God, but the rest pelted the embers at each other. Then they ran back to the forges and set them alight. Soon the whole island was like a blazing furnace and the sea hissed like a cauldron of stew boiling over a good fire. All day a long drawn-out wail could be heard. An intolerable, fetid stench emanated from the island and was still perceptible after they had lost sight of it. Brendan tried to comfort his flock: 'Soldiers of Christ, put on spiritual arms and stand firm in faith unfeigned. Watch and play the man, for we are at hell's gates.'

24 The next day a high mountain came up towards the north. At a distance it seemed wreathed in light cloud, but the cloud turned out to be smoke belching from its peak. The wind carried them swiftly towards it. The cliffs at the water's edge were so high that the summit was obscured; they were as black as coal and wonderfully sheer, like a wall.

One of the three monks who had followed Brendan out of the monastery suddenly leapt overboard and started wading to the bottom of the cliffs, calling out: 'Woe is me, father, I am being torn away from you and am powerless to turn back.' The monks hastily pushed the boat off, crying out to the Lord: 'Have mercy upon us O Lord, have mercy!' Then they witnessed the wretch being led off to torment by a group of devils. He and they would burn together. 'Woe to you, my son!' exclaimed Brendan. 'What a dreadful doom you have brought upon yourself.' A fair wind carried them away southwards, and, when they looked back from afar, they saw the mountain, clear of clouds, vomiting forth flames sky-high and then sucking them back upon itself, so that the whole mass of rock, right down to sea-level, glowed like a pyre.

25 Seven days after this fearful sight, St Brendan espied a shape

in the sea that looked like a man perched on a rock. A length
of cloth, the size of a cloak, hung down in front of it from
two spits. The whole thing was being battered by the waves
like a skiff in a whirlpool. Some of the monks said it was a
bird, others a ship. 'Put an end to the discussion,' said Brendan, 'and turn the boat towards it.'

As Brendan approached, the waves retreated as though
turned to jelly, revealing a swarthy and disfigured man
crouching on the rock. When the waves surged in, they
crashed right over his head, and when they retreated the rock
stood out stark and bare. The sheet of cloth would alternately
billow out, leaving him exposed to the gale and then, caught
by the wind, would lash in and smack him hard about the
face and eyes.

The saintly abbot asked him who he was and what crime
he could have committed to have deserved such a fate.

'I am of all men the most wretched,' came the answer, 'for
I am Judas Iscariot who foully bargained away the life of his
Master. Jesus Christ's unspeakable mercy, not my own desert,
has put me here. To me this is no place of punishment. It is
the spot where my loving Saviour grants me respite in honour
of His Resurrection. Sitting here is like being in the Garden
of Delights, compared to the torments to which I can look
forward this evening. My punishment is to burn like a lump
of molten lead in a crucible, day and night, in the middle of
yonder mountain, the home of Leviathan* and his allies. I
was there when that brother of yours was swallowed up. The
mountain shot out great flames then, as though leaping for
joy – that is the usual welcome for a damned soul. I come
here to rest from first to second vespers of every Sunday, from
Christmas to Epiphany, from Easter to Whitsun, and on the
feasts of the Purification and the Assumption of the Mother
of God. The rest of the year I am torn in hell with Herod and
Pilate, Annas and Caiaphas. I implore you, therefore, to beg
Our Lord Jesus Christ, the Redeemer of the World, to let me
stay here till sunrise tomorrow, so that the devils may not take
your arrival as a sign to come to torture me and drag me off
to the destiny I purchased at so horrible a price.'

* Biblical monster (*Job* 41, *Isaiah* 27).

'God's will be done,' the saint replied, 'the devils will not gnaw you till morning. But tell me, what is that cloth for?'

'It is a sheet I gave a leper when I was the Lord's treasurer, but since it was not mine to give – it belonged to Him and His brethren – it is more hindrance than help to me now. These iron spits to which the cloth is tied are those I gave the temple priests as a stand for cooking pots. This rock I sit on used to lie in the open street, where I flung it into the gutter to trip up passers-by, before I became His disciple.'

No sooner had twilight begun to close in over the deep than a vast cloud of demons wheeled about, yelling at the top of their voice: 'Keep out of our way, man of God! We cannot reach our colleague if you stay close to him, and, without him, we dare not face our prince. So give us our tasty morsel, do not shield him from us tonight.'

'It is not I who shield him, but the Lord Jesus Christ. He has granted him respite here until tomorrow morning.'

'How can you invoke the Lord's name over His own betrayer?'

'I command you,' Brendan retorted, 'in the name of that same Jesus Christ, not to lay hands on him till tomorrow.'

Once night was past and the man of God had set sail, an endless press of demons covered the face of the deep, yelling hideously and calling out: 'O man of God, cursed be your goings out and your comings in! All night long we have been flogged with the utmost severity for not bringing our prince that damned slave.'

'Your maledictions shall light on yourselves, not on us; for whomsoever you curse is blessed, and cursed is he whom you bless.'

'Because you shielded him from us last night, he shall receive twice as much punishment these next six days.'

'Neither you nor your leader have power to do so; that decision lies with God. Therefore I command both you and him, in the name of Our Lord Jesus Christ, to torment Judas no more severely than before.'

'Why should we take notice of what you say? Do you think you are Lord of all?'

'No. I have no power except what God has given me, but I

am His servant and whatever I command in His name shall be done.'

The demons followed Brendan till Judas was out of sight, then they turned back and violently snatched away the miserable wretch with a loud plangent cry.

26 St Brendan and his co-warriors in Christ sailed away in a southerly direction, glorifying God in all things. The appearance of a small island in the distance towards the south made them row more spiritedly. 'Do not row too fast,' Brendan advised them, as they were approaching it. 'You will soon tire yourselves out. You have toiled quite enough – this coming Easter will mark the seventh anniversary of our leaving our homeland. In a short time you will meet Paul the Hermit, a very holy man. He has lived on that island for the past sixty years without a mouthful of food. For thirty years before that an animal used to bring him food.'

The cliffs were so sheer that it was impossible to find a landing place. The island itself was small and round, about a furlong in circumference and as high as it was wide. On top of the cliffs there was no soil, only bare, jagged flint. They sailed round and round and came upon a narrow harbour, barely wide enough to let the prow of the boat pass through. They had difficulty in clambering out of the boat. 'Wait here,' Brendan instructed them, 'till I return. You may not have access to the island without first obtaining permission from the servant of God who dwells here.'

He climbed up to the summit and saw two caves with their mouths facing each other, on the eastern side of the isle, and a tiny spring gushing out from a rock in front of the mouth of the cave where the soldier of Christ was sitting. The spring water, as it fell, was at once absorbed by the rock. While Brendan was peering into the mouth of one cave, the old hermit emerged from the cave opposite, saying: 'Behold how good and joyful it is for brethren to dwell together in unity.' Paul told Brendan to call the monks up from the coracle, kissed them when they arrived, and addressed them each by name. This prophetic gift of knowing their names added to their astonishment at his attire: he wore no clothes at all, yet only his face and eyes were visible, the rest of his body being covered from head to foot with his hair, beard and body hair – all of which was snow white on account of his age. Brendan felt sad within himself at the sight : 'How ashamed I feel, I who wear the habit of a monk and have jurisdiction over many monks in our order, when I see this mortal man living like an angel and wholly free from the sins of the flesh.'

'Venerable father,' the hermit replied, 'God has worked many astounding miracles on your behalf, such as have never been vouchsafed to any of the holy fathers. You say you are not worthy to wear the habit of a monk, yet you are higher than any monk. A monk has to support himself by the sweat of his brow, but, for the past seven years, God has secretly fed and clothed you and your family of monks.'

In answer to Brendan's questions where he had come from, how he had come and how long he had borne so hard a life, Paul replied : 'For forty years I was brought up in St Patrick's monastery, where I was caretaker of the cemetery. One day the prior told me to dig a grave in a certain spot for one of the monks. As I was digging, an old man, whom I did not recognize, came up to me and said: "Do not dig the grave there, brother. That plot of ground is for someone else."

' "Who are you, father ? " I asked.

' "What ! Do you not know me ? Do you not recognize your abbot ? "

' "St Patrick is my abbot," I answered.

' "I am he," the apparition replied. "Yesterday I departed this life and here I am to be buried." He pointed to another spot. "Dig a grave here for the brother who has died recently, and do not repeat what I have told you. Go down to the shore tomorrow and you will find a small boat waiting. Step into it and it will take you to the place where you are to await the day of your death."

'The following morning I went down to the shore and found a boat, just as St Patrick had said. I boarded it and sailed for three days and nights. From the fourth day onward I let myself sail with the wind and on the seventh day I sighted this island and the vessel came straight towards it. Once landed I pushed the boat off with my foot and back it went to my native land, furrowing swiftly through the waves. And here I have remained. Every third day, at the ninth hour, a sea-otter would emerge from the water on its hind legs, with a fish for my dinner in its mouth and a small bundle of twigs between its front paws for kindling a fire. It put down the fish and the bundle of twigs and returned to the sea. I lit a fire with flint and iron and cooked the fish. For thirty years the otter fed me. I ate a third part of the fish each day and, thank God, never experienced thirst, for on Sundays a trickle of water flowed from a rock. This provided me with drink there and then and I used to fill a flask to last me for the rest of the week. I did not discover these two caves nor the spring until I had been here thirty years. From then on I lived – indeed am still living – on spring water and nothing else. I have lived ninety years on this island – for thirty of which I lived on fish, and the remaining sixty on water from this spring – and I was fifty when I left my own country; so I am now one hundred and forty years old. And here, in this mortal flesh, I shall soon see my judgement day dawn. Away you go now, and fill your bottles at the spring. You will need water: you have a forty-day journey ahead of you between now and Holy Saturday. You will celebrate Holy Saturday and Easter Sunday and its octave in the same places as you have done these past six years. But this time, when you have received your steward's blessing, you will journey to the Land of Promise of the Saints, and after forty days spent there the God of your fathers will bring you back safe and sound to the land of your birth.'

27 St Brendan and his monks received the old man's blessing and set off southwards. During the whole of Lent their little barque was carried hither and thither over the ocean and their only source of nourishment was the water they had brought with them from Paul the Hermit's isle. Yet they were quite content: one drink every three days perfectly satisfied their appetite for food and drink.

On Holy Saturday they arrived at the island where their steward was waiting for them. He was so overjoyed to see them that he lifted them bodily out of the coracle, one by one.

When the office of the day was over, he set before them a meal, and on the evening of that same day they put to sea again, taking the steward with them.

They found Jasconius in the usual place, climbed out on to his back, and sang to the Lord the whole night, and said their masses the next morning. After the last mass, the whale swam away and all the brethren called out : 'Hear us, O God of our salvation, thou that art the hope of all the ends of the earth, and of them that remain in the broad sea.'

'Have no fear,' said Brendan, trying to comfort them, 'The beast will not harm you; it is helping us on our way.'

The whale swam in a straight line towards the Island of Birds, and there they stayed till the octave of Pentecost.

When the solemn season had ended, the steward said to Brendan: 'Fill your water-bottles from this spring here and go back on board. This time I shall be your guide and companion, for without me you will never find the Land of Promise of the Saints.' As they left, all the birds called out : 'May the God of our salvation grant you a safe journey !'

28 The steward took them back to his island and stocked up the coracle with all they would need on the forty days' journey east which they were about to undertake. He led the way, sailing on in front of them. On the evening of the fortieth day they were enveloped in darkness, so thick that they could hardly see each other. 'Do you know what this darkness is ?' the steward asked.

'No,' said Brendan.

'It swirls round that island which you have been seeking these seven long years.' An hour later a brilliant light shone round them – their boat had reached the shore. Before them lay open country covered with apple trees laden with fruit. The monks ate as much as they wanted and drank deeply from the springs. The island was so wide that forty days' wandering still did not bring them to the farther shore. One day they came upon a vast river flowing through the middle of the country. 'What are we to do ?' asked Brendan. 'We have no idea of the size of the country and we cannot cross this river.' While he was standing pondering, a young man approached, kissed the monks joyfully, called them each by name, and said: 'Blessed are they that dwell in thy house, O Lord. They shall praise thee for ever and ever.'

He turned to Brendan. 'Now, at last, you have found the land you have been seeking all these years. The Lord Jesus Christ did not allow you to find it immediately, because first He wished to show you the richness of His wonders in the deep. Fill your ship brim-full with precious stones and return to the land of your birth. The day of your final journey is at hand; you shall soon be laid to rest with your fathers. After many more years have rolled by, this island will be revealed to your successors at the time when Christians will be undergoing persecution. This river divides the island in two. You must be thinking that it is autumn and the fruit has just ripened – it is like this the whole year round; dusk and darkness are unknown, for Christ Himself is our light.'

They gathered fruit and all kinds of gems, bade the young man farewell, dismissed their steward with a blessing, and sailed away into the belt of darkness. Once they had passed beyond it, they soon came to the Island of Delights. After a three days' stay they set off, with the abbot's blessing, on a direct route for their own monastery.

29 Brendan's community was rapturous with joy at his return, and glorified God for His kindness in letting them once more enjoy the sight of their father from whom they had been separated so long. St Brendan returned their affection and recounted everything he remembered of the voyage and all the wonders God had deigned to show him. Finally he informed them of the prophecy made by the young man on the Island of Promise, assuring them that he had not long to live. Events proved him right; he put all his affairs in order, and very shortly afterwards, fortified with the sacraments of the Church, lay back in the arms of his disciples and gave up his illustrious spirit to the Lord, to whom be honour and glory, world without end. Amen.

The end

# Bede: Life of Cuthbert

*The prologue of the holy priest Bede to the*
Life of Saint Cuthbert


To my holy and most blessed lord and father, Bishop Eadfrid, and to the whole congregation of monks serving God at Lindisfarne, Bede, your faithful servant, sends greeting. It is on your orders that I am writing this customary kind of preface – to let the reader know that the task of writing the book itself was undertaken in brotherly compliance with your wishes. I should also like to inform him, at this point, about what he might otherwise remain ignorant of, and to remind yourselves that I have written nothing about the saint without first subjecting the facts to the most thorough scrutiny and have passed on nothing to be transcribed for general reading that has not been obtained by rigorous examination of trustworthy witnesses. Indeed, before ever beginning to write, I carried out a thorough investigation of the whole of the saint's glorious life, with the help of those who had actually known him. I occasionally mention some of their names in the body of the book so that you can see for yourselves exactly what the sources are.

While the book was still in note form, it was often looked over and revised by our very reverend brother, the priest Herefrith, whenever he came here, and by others who had lived a long time with the man of God, and who were, therefore, more conversant with the details of his life. On their advice I made several amendments. I have tried to avoid all ambiguity or hair-splitting and to write a clear investigation of the truth in simple terms. I have already taken care to let you yourselves examine what I have written, so that what was false could be amended, what was true, confirmed.

When, with the help of the Lord, the book was finished, and had been read for two days before the elders and doctors of your community, and its every detail had been considered, they then approved all I had written, declaring it fit to be

read and transcribed by all whose holy zeal moved them to
do so. The discussions you held among yourselves have
brought to light many other facts, just as important as those
I record here and well worth writing down, except that it
hardly seems right to make insertions and add to a carefully
planned and completed work. Furthermore, since I have been
quick to carry out the task you thought fit to impose on me,
may I suggest you crown your kindness by not being slow
to reward me by your prayers. When, in reading my book,
your hearts are raised to a more burning desire for the Kingdom of Heaven, by the memory of our holy father, do not
forget to intercede with the divine mercy on behalf of one
so small, so that I may be found worthy on earth to long for
and hereafter in perfect bliss to see 'the goodness of the Lord
in the land of the living'. And, when I am dead, pray for
my soul and say mass for me as though I were one of your
own household, and be so good as to inscribe my name on the
roll with your own.

You, my lord bishop, will recall having already promised
me this; in witness whereof you ordered our holy brother,
Godfrith, the sacristan, to put my name in the register of
your congregation even now. You may be aware, holy father,
that I have already produced, at the request of some of the
brothers here, a life of this same father of ours, in heroic
verse, somewhat shorter than this prose life but following
the same pattern. You may, if you wish, have a copy. In the
preface to the verse life I promised that I would later write
a fuller account of the life and miracles, a promise which, as
far as God permits, I am now striving to fulfil. On behalf
of our congregation, beloved brethren and masters, I pray
that the Almighty Lord may keep you secure in bliss.

Amen

### CHAPTER I

*How the holy child Cuthbert was warned by an infant
and told that he would be a bishop*

THE beginning of our account of the life and miracles of the
blessed Cuthbert is consecrated by the words which the

prophet Jeremiah uses of the state of perfection of the hermit:
'It is good for a man to have borne the yoke in his youth; he
shall sit in solitude and be silent, because he will raise himself
above himself'; for it was the sweetness of this way of life
which led Cuthbert, in his earliest youth, to put his neck
to the yoke of monastic discipline. Later, when the opportunity arose, he embraced the hermit's life and lived a long
while in silence, pleased to forgo the speech of men for the
delights of divine contemplation. To fit him for these tasks
the grace of God urged him on, little by little, in the way
of truth from his earliest years. Up to his eighth year, the end
of infancy and the threshold of boyhood, he had no mind
for anything but games and carefree play, so that what was
said of Samuel might well be said of him: 'He did not yet
know the Lord, neither was the word of the Lord revealed
unto him.' This is as a prelude to my praise of his boyhood.
Later he came to know the Lord perfectly and opened the
ear of his heart to receive His word.

He loved games and pranks, and as was natural at his age,
loved to play with other children. He was naturally agile and
quick-witted and usually won the game. He would often be
still fresh when the rest were tired and would look round
in triumph, as though the game were in his hands, and ask
who was willing to continue. He used to boast that he had
beaten all those of his own age and many who were older at
wrestling, jumping, running, and every other exercise. For
'when he was a child, he understood as a child', but when a
man, 'he put away childish things'. And Providence chose a
very suitable way of checking his childish ardour. Bishop
Trumwine of happy memory tells the story as he had it from
Cuthbert himself:

One day a great crowd of lads were at their usual games in
a field, Cuthbert among them, twisting themselves about in
all kinds of contortions in the excitement of the game. Suddenly a child no more than three years old ran up to him and
began to upbraid him, with all the solemnity of an old man,
for his idleness and indulgence in games, saying he would do
better to exercise a steady control over mind and body. When
Cuthbert ridiculed the idea, the child threw himself wailing

to the ground, the tears pouring down his cheeks. The others rushed to comfort him, asking why he had suddenly burst into tears, but to no avail. When Cuthbert himself tried to cheer him up, he cried out: 'Why, most holy priest and bishop Cuthbert, do you persist in doing what is so contrary both to your nature and your rank? How ill it befits you to play with children, you whom the Lord has marked out to instil virtue into your elders!'

Cuthbert took this good-naturedly, listened indeed with rapt attention, and soothed the child's feelings with a friendly show of affection. He forsook his foolish games at once and went home. From then on he showed himself more mature and earnest, as the Spirit, who had spoken to him through the mouth of an infant, spoke to him now in the recesses of his heart.

Let it not cause astonishment that God should check the folly of a child by a child. Did He not, when He thought fit, restrain the foolishness of a prophet by putting human words into the mouth of an ass? One can truly say in His praise, 'Out of the mouths of babes and sucklings Thou hast perfected praise.'

### CHAPTER 2

*How he was lamed by a disease of the knee and immediately cured by an angel*

IT is a true saying that 'unto everyone that hath shall be given, and he shall have abundance' – that is, whoever has his mind set on virtue shall be greatly endowed with virtues from above. The child Cuthbert, as a reward for carefully storing up in his heart the advice given him by human means, was privileged to see and talk with an angel. His knee suddenly began to hurt and a great tumour swelled up, causing the muscles of the knee-cap to contract. At first he could manage to hop with his foot off the ground, but the swelling got so much worse that he could hardly walk at all. One day the servants carried him outside to lie in the fresh air. Looking up he caught sight of a horseman approaching from afar, dressed in white, with noble looks, on a steed of unparalleled beauty. He rode up, saluted him courteously, and asked, almost jokingly, if he would mind ministering to a guest such as him. Cuthbert replied: 'I am only too ready to devote myself to showing you hospitality, but I am pinned down, for my sins, by this weakness of the leg. I have been troubled with it for a long time now and there is no doctor anywhere with skill enough to cure it.'

The horseman alighted, looked hard at the knee, and said: 'Boil some wheaten flour in milk and bathe the tumour with it hot, and you will be healed.'

He mounted and rode off. Cuthbert did as he was bidden and within a few days was well again. Then he knew that it was an angel that had given him the remedy, sent by the same power who had deigned to send the Archangel Raphael to cure Tobias's eyes. If anyone thinks it strange for an angel to appear on horseback, let him read the history of the Maccabees, where angels on horseback come to defend both Judas Maccabeus and the Temple itself.

## CHAPTER 3

*How the winds changed at his prayer and the rafts, which had been carried away, were brought back safe to land*

HENCEFORTH the boy devoted himself to God, and, as he would later recount to his friends, when he prayed for help against frequent and pressing difficulties, he often had angels sent to defend him. He was heard by Him who is wont to listen to the cry of the poor and deliver them from all their tribulations, because he in turn was kind enough to pray for others in similar dangers.

There is a monastery near the mouth of the Tyne,* on the south bank, once full of monks, but changed, like everything else, by the course of time, and now housing a noble company of women. These monks used to bring the wood they needed for the house by raft, from a good distance away along the current of the river. One day they had reached the point opposite the monastery and were bringing the rafts in

* At Jarrow.

when a sudden gale rose out of the west, scattered the rafts, and dragged them down towards the mouth of the river. The monks inside the monastery saw what had happened and launched out to help their brethren labouring on the rafts; but the fury of the wind got the better of them and they could do nothing. Giving up hope of human aid they fled to the divine – while the rafts were floating out to sea, they came out of the monastery, gathered round the nearest rock and prayed fervently to the Lord for their brethren who were on the point of perishing before their very eyes. The answer to their prayers was long delayed, but when it did come it was clearly the work of God's providence, manifesting the power of Cuthbert's prayers. He himself was standing on the opposite bank of the river among a great crowd of peasants. The rafts floating out to sea looked like five birds bobbing up and down on the waves. While the monks opposite were watching in sorrow, the peasants began to jeer at their way of life, as though they deserved such misfortune for spurning the life of the ordinary man and introducing new, unheard-of rules of conduct. Cuthbert stopped their insults.

'Do you realize what you are doing ? Would it not be more human of you to pray for their safety rather than to gloat over their misfortune ? '

But they, boors both in thought and speech, fulminated against him.

'Nobody is going to pray for them. Let not God raise a finger to help them! They have done away with all the old ways of worship* and now nobody knows what to do.'

The saint listened to them and then knelt down and prayed, bending low to the ground. At once the wind changed right about and bore them safe and sound to land at a very convenient spot beside the monastery. Seeing this, the country people burnt inwardly with shame at their impiety. They gave due credit to Cuthbert's faith, and from then on never ceased to praise him. The man who told me the story, a worthy brother of this monastery, said he had often heard one of that very group, a simple peasant, incapable of lying, tell the tale before a large audience.

*i.e. pagan worship.

## CHAPTER 4

*How, when he was with some shepherds, he saw the soul of
St Aidan borne heavenward by angels*

WHEN Christ, by whose grace the lives of the faithful are
directed and guided, decided to call his servant to a higher
and harder way of life, to earn a greater and more glorious
reward, Cuthbert, at the time, happened to be looking after
a flock of sheep committed to his charge, away up in the hills.
One night when his companions had gone to sleep and he
was keeping watch and praying as usual, he suddenly saw
light streaming from the skies, breaking the long night's
darkness, and the choirs of the heavenly host coming down
to earth. They quickly took into their ranks a human soul,
marvellously bright, and returned to their home above. The
youth was moved by this vision to give himself to spiritual
discipline in order to gain eternal happiness with the mighty
men of God. There and then he set about thanking God
and exhorting his companions in a brotherly way to praise
Him.

'What wretches we are, given up to sleep and sloth so that
we never see the glory of those who watch with Christ unceasingly! After so short a vigil what marvels have I seen!
The gate of Heaven opened and a band of angels led in the
spirit of some holy man. While we are still in the deepest
darkness, he has the happiness of looking forever on the halls
of heaven and their King. I think he must have been some
holy bishop or layman of great distinction since he was led
in with such splendour and light by retinues of angels.'

In this way Cuthbert fired the hearts of the shepherds
with the love and honour of God. Next day he was told that
Aidan, Bishop of Lindisfarne, a man of outstanding holiness,
had passed into the Kingdom of Heaven at the time of his
vision. He delivered the sheep back to their owners and decided to enter a monastery.

## CHAPTER 5

*How God provided food for him on a journey*

WHILE he was seriously contemplating entering on a higher
course of life, he received a great grace to strengthen his
resolve, and, incidentally, to show quite clearly that those
who seek the Kingdom of Heaven and its justice will, by the
mercy of providence, not lack bodily sustenance. He was
travelling alone one day and, about the third hour, chanced
to turn into a distant village. He went to the home of a devout
married woman, wishing to rest a while; he was more
worried about food for his horse than for himself, for winter
was just beginning. The woman made him welcome and
pressed him to let her prepare him a meal. But the saint
would not permit it; he could not eat as it was a Friday, a
day on which many of the faithful, in honour of the Death
of our Lord, are wont to prolong their fast till the ninth
hour. The woman, being hospitality's own self, insisted.

'You will not find another village on your way, nor even
a house; and it will take you till sunset to reach your destination. At least take something with you, otherwise you will
be fasting the whole day, perhaps even till tomorrow.' But
his zeal for religion got the better of her insistence and he set
out still fasting and remained in that state till vespers. When
it came to vesper time he saw that he would not be able to
finish the journey that day; he saw too that there was no
human dwelling within reach. He suddenly noticed some
shepherds' huts, very makeshift constructions, built for the
summer, and deserted. He went in, meaning to stay the
night, tied the horse to the wall, and gave it a bunch of straw
he had gathered from bits blown out of the roof. He passed
the time in prayer. Looking up from his psalms he saw the
horse lift its head up and start to pull straw out of the roof.
Suddenly a bundle wrapped in a linen cloth fell down with
the straw. When his prayers were over he got up to find out
what it was and discovered half a loaf still warm and some
meat wrapped in the cloth, enough for one meal.

'O God,' he said, 'I was fasting for the love of Thee and in return Thou hast fed both me and my animal, blessed be Thy Name.'

He broke the bread and gave half to the horse. From that day on he was much more ready to fast, now that he knew he had been fed in his solitude by Him who, when there was no one else to provide, had sent the very birds, day after day, with food for Elijah in the wilderness. His eyes are ever on them that fear Him and hope in His mercy, so that He may, in the words of the Psalmist, 'snatch their souls from death and feed them in time of famine.' The holy priest Ingwald from our monastery at Monkwearmouth heard this from Cuthbert when the latter was a bishop. Ingwald, thanks to his ripe old age, has ceased to gaze on earthly things with the eyes of the flesh; his heart is completely taken up with the things of Heaven.

## CHAPTER 6

*Boisil's prophecy. Cuthbert arrives at Melrose,*
*is welcomed and remains there*

OUR venerable servant of God, meanwhile, was hastening to leave the world and take upon himself monastic discipline. Spurred on by his heavenly vision of the joys of eternal bliss, he was ready to suffer hunger and thirst in this life in order to enjoy the banquets of the next. The community of Lindisfarne, he knew, was well adorned with holy monks, under whose example and teaching he might make good progress, but the reputation for sublime virtue enjoyed by Boisil, priest of Melrose, led him to enter there. By chance Boisil was standing at the monastery gates when he arrived and thus saw him first. Cuthbert dismounted, gave his horse and spear to a servant (he had not yet put off secular dress), and went into the church to pray. Boisil had an intuition of the high degree of holiness to which the boy he had just been looking at would rise, and said just this single phrase to the monks with whom he was standing: 'Behold the servant of the Lord,' imitating Him who, at the approach of Nathaniel, exclaimed: 'Behold an Israelite indeed, one in whom there is no guile'. An old veteran, Sigfrith, priest of Jarrow monastery, told me the tale; he was there with Boisil at the time, a mere youth in the first steps of the monastic life. Now he is living the life of perfection. He has only a few feeble breaths left in him and is thirsting for the joys of the future life.

Boisil said no more. He welcomed Cuthbert and when he explained the purpose of his visit, namely to leave the world behind him. Boisil received him with great kindness into the community. Boisil himself was prior. A few days later the priest Eata arrived, then Abbot of Melrose and later Abbot and Bishop of Lindisfarne. Boisil told him about Cuthbert, explained how well disposed he was, and gained permission for him to receive the tonsure and become one of the community. Once admitted, Cuthbert was careful to keep up with the rest in observing the rule. He excelled them in zeal for strict discipline. He watched, prayed, worked, and read harder than anyone else. Like Samson the Nazarite he carefully abstained from all alcoholic drink, but he was not so severe with himself as regards food lest his work should suffer. He was robust and strong, fit enough to carry out everything he chose to put his hand to.

## CHAPTER 7

*How he entertained an angel and, in seeking to give him*
*earthly food, was rewarded in turn with bread from heaven*

A FEW years later when King Alhfrith, for the salvation of his soul, gave Abbot Eata ground at Ripon\* to build a monastery, the abbot transferred some of the monks to live there, under the same rule as they had at Melrose. Cuthbert was one of them. He was appointed guestmaster and is said to have had an angel sent to him as a guest to test his devotion.

One morning he left the inner monastery buildings to go

---

\* When Eata showed himself unwilling to accept Roman practices, Alhfrith drove him and his Celtic monks away from Ripon, and gave the land and monastery to Wilfrid (*Cuthbert*, Chapter 8; and *Wilfrid*, Chapter 8).

to the guest chamber and found a youth sitting inside. He
gave him the usual sort of kindly welcome, thinking, naturally, that he was a man. He got him water to wash his hands,
washed his feet himself, dried them, put them in his bosom,
and humbly chafed them with his hands. The youth was
asked to wait till after terce, when a meal would be ready;
otherwise if he left at once he would faint with hunger in
the winter cold. He thought the lad had travelled all night
through the wind and snow and had put in at the monastery
at dawn to rest. But the youth said he must leave immediately and hurry to a far distant place. Cuthbert asked question after question and finally adjured him in God's Name
to stay. As soon as terce was over it was dinner time, and
a table was set and food brought.

'Now eat and get your strength back,' Cuthbert urged him,
'while I go and get you some warm bread. I hope it will be
ready.'

When he came back the youth had vanished. The ground
was covered with fresh snow but there were no footsteps to
be seen. The man of God was amazed. He puzzled over what
had happened and then went to put the table back in the
storehouse. At the door there was a wonderfully fragrant
odour. He looked about to see where it was coming from and
there beside him were three loaves, unusually white and fine.
Trembling he said to himself: 'Now I know that it was an
angel, come not to be fed but to feed. He has brought bread
such as cannot be produced on earth, whiter than the lily,
sweeter than roses, more delicious than honey. Such food, it
is obvious, comes not from this world of ours but from the
paradise of joy. No wonder he refused human food when he
can enjoy in Heaven the bread of eternal life.' The manifest
virtue of this miracle moved the saint to even greater zeal for
good works, and as his virtues increased, so did the grace
that was given him. Angels would often appear and talk with
him and when he was hungry he would be refreshed with
food by the special gift of God. Cuthbert was a very pleasant,
affable man; he generally restricted himself to citing the lives
of the fathers when he wanted to find models of godly living
for his brethren, yet sometimes, in all humility, he would

mention his own spiritual graces. Sometimes he did this
openly, sometimes he talked in the third person as though
it were someone else. His audience always knew that he
was speaking like St Paul, who at times would recount his
virtues openly, at times as though speaking of another –
when, for example, he says: 'I knew a man in Christ, above
fourteen years ago, such an one caught up even to the seventh
heaven,' and so on.

## CHAPTER 8

*How Cuthbert was cured of a disease, and how the dying
Boisil prophesied what was in store for him*

ALL the ways of this world are as fickle and unstable as a
sudden storm at sea. Eata and Cuthbert and all the rest were
thrown out of Ripon and the monastery they had built was
given over to other monks. This change of place did not
weaken our athlete of Christ in his determination once taken
to do battle for Heaven. He followed the words and actions
of Boisil with undiminished fervour, but he was struck down
about this time by a plague which was ravaging the length
and breadth of the country. (My source for this is Herefrith,
a priest of the saint's own community and later Bishop of
Lindisfarne, who had the story from Cuthbert himself.) The
monks spent the whole night in prayer, for they felt they
could not do without him on account of his holiness. His
reply the next morning when one of the monks mentioned
the vigil – for they had kept it quiet from him – was: 'Then
what am I lying here for? God will certainly have heard the
prayers of so many good men. Fetch me my shoes and stick.'
He got up there and then and tried to walk with the stick.
Day by day his strength came back until he was quite
recovered; only the swelling on the thigh seemed to move
inwards, and for almost the whole of his life he was troubled
with some internal pain, so that, to quote the apostle,
'strength was made perfect in weakness'.

Boisil saw that he was better and prophesied that he would
never again be stricken by the same malady. 'At the same
time,' said Boisil, 'I warn you not to lose the chance of

learning from me, for death is upon me. By next week my body and voice shall have lost their strength.'

Cuthbert knew that he was telling the truth.

'Then tell me what is the best book to study, one that can be got through in a week.'

'St John the Evangelist,' Boisil answered. 'I have a commentary in seven parts. With the help of God we can read one a day and perhaps discuss it if we want.'

It was done as he said. They were able to finish quickly because they dealt not with the profound arguments but with the simple things of 'the faith which worketh by love'. On the seventh day, when the reading was finished, illness overtook Boisil, and – this I recount with gladness – he entered into the joy of eternal bliss. He is believed to have unfolded all Cuthbert's future during that week. He was a prophet and a very holy man. Three years before the epidemic came he foretold it to Abbot Eata and did not conceal the fact that he would perish. Eata, he said, would not be carried off but would die of what the doctors called dysentery. His prophecy turned out right. He hinted to Cuthbert that he would be a bishop. Afterwards, when he was living a hermit's life, Cuthbert would not mention the predicted honour, except occasionally to his brethren.

'If,' he would lament, 'I could live in a tiny dwelling on a rock in the ocean, surrounded by the swelling waves, cut off from the knowledge and the sight of all, I would still not be free from the cares of this fleeting world nor from the fear that somehow the love of money might snatch me away.'

## CHAPTER 9

*How Cuthbert was most assiduous in preaching the word*

ON Boisil's death Cuthbert became prior, an office which he carried out for many years with holy zeal. Inside the monastery he counselled the monks on the religious life and set a high example of it himself, and outside, in the world, he strove to convert people for miles around from their foolish

ways to a delight in the promised joys of Heaven. Many
who had the faith had profaned it by their works. Even while
the plague was raging some had forgotten the mystery
conferred on them in baptism and had fled to idols, as though
incantations or amulets or any other diabolical rubbish could
possibly avail against a punishment sent by God the Creator.
To bring back both kinds of sinners he often did the rounds
of the villages, sometimes on horseback, more often on foot,
preaching the way of truth to those who had gone astray.
Boisil did the same in his time. It was the custom at that time
among the English people that if a priest or cleric came to
a village everyone would obey his call and gather round to
hear him preach. They would willingly listen and even more
gladly put his words into practice as far as they had understood them. Such was his skill in teaching, such his power
of driving his lessons home, and so gloriously did his angelic
countenance shine forth, that none dared keep back from him
even the closest secrets of their heart. They confessed every
sin openly – indeed they thought he would know if they held
anything back – and made amends by 'fruits worthy of re-
pentance', as he commanded. He made a point of searching
out those steep rugged places in the hills which other preach-
ers dreaded to visit because of their poverty and squalor.
This, to him, was a labour of love. He was so keen to preach
that sometimes he would be away for a whole week or a
fortnight, or even a month, living with the rough hill folk,
preaching and calling them heavenwards by his example.

### CHAPTER 10

*How after he had spent the whole night praying in the sea,
animals ministered unto him as he came out of the water, and
how one of the monks, ill with fear at the sight, was restored
by his prayers*

INSIDE the monastery the man of God performed more and
more signs and wonders, and his reputation kept pace. There
was a nun called Aebbe, a real mother to the Lord's handmaids, in charge of the convent of Coldingham, honoured

for piety and nobility alike, for she was King Oswiu's sister. She sent to Cuthbert to ask if he would come and exhort the community. So kind a request could not be refused. He came and stayed a few days, showing them the way of righteousness in deed as well as word. He was in the habit of rising at the dead of night, while everyone else was sleeping, to go out and pray, returning just in time for morning prayers. One night one of the monks watched him creep out, then followed him stealthily to see where he was going and what he was about. Down he went towards the beach beneath the monastery and out into the sea until he was up to his arms and neck in deep water. The splash of the waves accompanied his vigil throughout the dark hours of the night. At daybreak he came out, knelt down on the sand, and prayed. Then two otters bounded out of the water, stretched themselves out before him, warmed his feet with their breath, and tried to dry him on their fur. They finished, received his blessing, and slipped back to their watery home. He was soon home and was in choir at the proper time with the rest of the monks. But the brother who had spied on him from the cliffs returned with faltering steps, fear-stricken and distressed. He prostrated himself before Cuthbert and, in tears, craved pardon for his stupidity and presumption, quite sure that Cuthbert knew the cause of his discomfort.

'Why, what is wrong, what have you done?' asked the saint. 'Have you been spying on my night's work? I will forgive you, but only if you promise not to tell anyone while I am still alive.'

In this he followed his Master, who, when He had revealed the glory of His Majesty on the mount, warned the disciples, saying: 'Tell no man until the Son of Man be risen again from the dead.' The brother promised, received a blessing, and was freed from the guilt and embarrassment he had so rashly incurred; but the silence he preserved while Cuthbert was living he more than made up for once the saint was dead.

## CHAPTER II

*How he promised a calm sea to some sailors cut off by a
storm and how his prayer for food was answered*

MEANWHILE the man of God began to grow strong in prophecy, foretelling the future and revealing to those near him
events that were happening elsewhere. Once he had to go
to the land of the Niduari, a tribe of Picts, to settle some business or other. Two of the brethren travelled with him by
boat. (One of them, who afterwards became a priest, brought
this miracle to general notice.) They arrived after Christmas,
hoping to take advantage of the calm sea and favourable
winds to return soon. For this reason they did not trouble
about provisions, but matters turned out very differently
from what they expected. No sooner had they landed than a
violent storm arose, cutting them off completely, and they lan-
guished for some days, hungry and cold. Cuthbert, however,
did not waste this leisure time in idleness, nor did he merely
sleep through it. Night after night was spent in prayer. The
Feast of Epiphany was approaching, and in his usual blithe
and affable way he tried to raise his companions' spirits :

'Why do we remain listless and unresourceful ?' he asked.
'We ought to be thinking over every possible way of saving
ourselves. The land is bleak with snow, clouds lour in the
sky, there is a gale raging and the sea is a fury of waves, we
are dying of hunger and there is no chance of human aid.
Then let us storm Heaven with prayers, asking that same
Lord who parted the Red Sea and fed His people in the desert
to take pity on us in our peril. I believe that, unless our faith
falters, He will not let us go fasting, today of all days, the day
which He has singled out for such wondrous proofs of His
majesty. Let us move on and look for the banquet He will
surely provide for us to keep His festival with joy.' He led
them to the bank where he usually spent the whole night
praying, and there they found three cuts of dolphin meat,
ready to cook, as though prepared by human hand. They
went down on their knees and thanked God.

'You see,' said Cuthbert, 'what comes of trusting and hoping in the Lord. He has given his servants food, and in giving them three lots has shown how much longer they are to stay here. Pick up the gifts Christ has sent us. Come, let us eat and refuse to be daunted.'

Three days of fierce storm were followed by a calm sea and a blue sky, and they were wafted home with fair winds following.

## CHAPTER 12

*How on a journey he foretold that provisions would be brought by an eagle*

HE had gone out one day to preach as usual, taking a boy with him for company. Long before reaching their destination they were tired out. Cuthbert said to the boy, to test him: 'Tell me, son, where do you intend to eat today? Will you be able to turn in at friends on the way?'

'I was thinking about that myself,' answered the lad. 'We did not bring anything with us when we set out, and there is no one to ask a meal from. We cannot cover the rest of the journey fasting, without doing ourselves an injury.'

'Learn to have constant faith and hope in the Lord,' answered Cuthbert. 'He who serves God shall never die of hunger.' He looked up and saw an eagle flying high overhead. 'Do you see that eagle up there? God is quite capable of sending us food by it.'

They were making their way along a river, talking about such things, when they suddenly saw the eagle settling down on the bank.

'There,' said the saint, 'is the servant I was telling you about. Run and see what God has sent and bring it back quickly.'

The boy brought back a big fish which the bird had just caught.

'What!' said the saint. 'Did you not give the servant its share? Cut it in two, quickly now, and give half to the bird.'

The boy did as he was told. They put in at the next village and had the rest boiled. They and the family who cooked it for them had a most enjoyable meal. Cuthbert preached to them and praised God for His bounty, for 'blessed is the man whose hope is in the Lord and who has not sought after vanity or idle folly'. Then they resumed their journey to those they had set out to teach.

## CHAPTER 13

*How, while preaching to the people, he foresaw that the devil would send a phantom fire, and how he put it out*

HE suddenly realized, while preaching the words of life to a great crowd in a small village, that the ancient enemy, the devil, was present, come to hinder his work of salvation. He set out at once in his sermon to forestall the plot he knew to be hatching. He suddenly interrupted his discourse with this warning:

'My dear brethren, whenever you hear the mysteries of the Kingdom of Heaven being preached, you must be on your guard to listen with complete attention and not let the devil distract you with foolish worries from hearing what concerns your eternal salvation: for he has a thousand crafty ways of harming you.'

He immediately took up the thread of the sermon. All at once that wicked enemy sent down mock fire on to a nearby house. Sheets of flame, fanned by the wind, seemed to sweep through the whole village, and the noise of their crackling rent the air. Cuthbert managed, with outstretched hands, to restrain a few of the villagers, but the rest, almost the whole crowd, leaped up and vied with each other in throwing water on the flames. But real water has no effect on phantom fire, and the blaze raged on, until through Cuthbert's prayers the father of lies fled, taking his false fire with him, into the empty air. The crowd came to their senses, knelt before Cuthbert and, red in the face with shame, begged pardon for their fickleness, saying that they knew now that the devil did not cease for even an hour in his warfare against man's salvation. Cuthbert strengthened the weak and irresolute and carried on with his exhortations.

CHAPTER 14

*How Cuthbert checked the flames of a house that
was really on fire*

ONE day on his travels – for, like the apostles, he went every-
where preaching the way of salvation – he came to the house
of a holy woman who was much given to good works. He
often visited her because she was his old nurse, indeed he
always called her mother. She lived towards the west of the
village. No sooner had he entered the place than a house in
the eastern quarter caught fire through carelessness and
began to blaze. A wind sprang up from the same direction,
tore away wisps of blazing straw from the roof, and scattered
them far and wide. As the fire got hotter it kept back the
men who were throwing water, finally forcing them to retreat. This holy woman ran back to her home in great consternation to find Cuthbert and implore him to pray; otherwise the whole village would be destroyed, her house with it.

'Do not worry, mother, keep calm. You and yours will be
safe, no matter how fierce the flame.'

He went out and lay full length on the ground in front
of the door. Before he had finished praying the wind had
changed to the west and put the house the man of God
had entered completely out of danger. In these two miracles
he imitated the wonders of two of the fathers. In foreseeing
and getting rid of phantom fire he followed the most holy
and reverend father Benedict, who cast out a fire kindled by
our ancient foe in the form of a burning kitchen, and in
extinguishing and changing the direction of great sheets of
flame he is comparable to the venerable Marcellinus, bishop
of Ancona. When that city was burning Marcellinus stationed
himself in front of the flames and damped them by prayer
when the efforts of the whole city had proved useless. No
wonder that the tried and faithful servants of God should
have power over ordinary fire; hard daily practice has taught
them both to subdue the fires of their own flesh and 'to
quench all the fiery darts of the wicked one'. The following

prophecy fits them aptly: 'When thou walkest through the fire thou shalt not be burned, neither shall the flame kindle upon thee.' Myself and those like me, knowing well our own weakness and helplessness, would not dare take any such measures against fire; we are not even sure of escaping scot-free from the undying fire of future punishment. But the loving kindness of Our Saviour is mighty and abundant. He will give us grace, unworthy though we are, to extinguish the flames of vice in this world, and escape the flames of punishment in the next.

### CHAPTER 15

*How he exorcised the wife of a sheriff even before*
*he reached her*

FROM having shown what power the venerable Cuthbert had against the deceits and frauds of the devil, we can now go on to reveal his strength in combating the fiend's undisguised fury. There was a sheriff of King Ecgfrith, called Hildmer, a man dedicated to good works along with all his household and therefore specially loved by Cuthbert. He visited Hildmer whenever he happened to be in the neighbourhood. His wife, though zealous in almsgiving and all the other fruits of virtue, was suddenly possessed of a devil. She was so sorely vexed that she would gnash her teeth, let out frightful howls, and fling her arms and legs about. It was terrifying to see or hear her. The convulsions gradually exhausted her, and she was already at death's door, or so it seemed, when her husband galloped off to fetch Cuthbert.

'My wife is ill,' he pleaded. 'She is very near her end. Send a priest before she goes, to give her the Body and Blood of the Lord and to bury her in holy ground.'

He was ashamed to admit that she whom Cuthbert was used to seeing well was now out of her mind. Cuthbert went off to see whom he could send when it suddenly came to him that she was in the grip of no ordinary illness; she was possessed. He returned.

'I will not send anyone else. I ought to go back with you and see her myself.'

As they were going along the sheriff began to weep. The bitterness of his anguish was apparent from the floods of tears. He was afraid that when Cuthbert found she was mad he might think she had served God up to now only in feigned faith. But the man of God gently soothed his fears.

'Do not weep. Your wife's condition will not astonish me. I know, even though you are ashamed to admit it, that she is afflicted by a demon. I know too that before I arrive the demon will have left her and that she herself will come running out to meet us as sound as ever. She will take the reins, bid us come in quickly, and treat us with all her usual attention. It is not only the wicked who are stricken down in this way. God, in his inscrutable designs, sometimes lets the innocent in this world be blighted by the devil, in mind as well as in body.'

Cuthbert continued to console and instruct his friend in this vein, and as they approached the house the evil spirit, unable to bear the coming of the Holy Spirit with whom Cuthbert was filled, suddenly departed. The woman, loosed from the chains of the devil, jumped up as though woken from a deep sleep, rushed out in gratitude to the saint, and caught hold of his bridle. Her bodily and mental strength soon returned completely. She asked him to dismount and come in to bless the house and waited on him with her most devoted attention. She admitted quite openly that at the first touch of his bridle all trace of her affliction had vanished.

CHAPTER 16

*How he lived and taught in the monastery at Lindisfarne*

WHEN the venerable servant of God had passed many years in the monastery at Melrose, where he had distinguished himself by many signs of spiritual power, Abbot Eata transferred him to the monastery at Lindisfarne, to teach the true rule of monastic life in his capacity as prior and to illustrate it by his own perfect example. Eata was Abbot of Lindisfarne too. Let no one be surprised to hear that Lindisfarne, as well as being an episcopal see (a fact which I have already mentioned), is also the home of an abbot and community, for indeed it is. The episcopal residence and the monastery are one and the same, and all the clergy are monks. Aidan, the first bishop, was a monk and he and his followers kept to the monastic life – hence every bishop of Lindisfarne has exercised his office in this way. The abbot, who is elected by the bishop and a council of monks, rules the monastery, while the clergy – priests, deacons, cantors, lectors, and the rest – live the full monastic life together with the bishop. Blessed Pope Gregory showed himself a great devotee of this way of life, as can be seen from the reference he makes in his reply to Augustine. He was the first bishop Gregory sent to the English and had written to ask what sort of life the clergy should lead. I quote from the letter: 'You, brother, have been brought up in the monastic rule. Now that the faith has been brought to the English you must not start living apart from your clergy. Introduce that way of life practised by the fathers of the early church, none of whom claimed as his own anything that he possessed – for everything was held in common.'

So when Cuthbert came to the church and monastery of Lindisfarne he handed on the monastic rule by teaching and example; moreover, he continued his custom of frequent visits to the common people in the neighbourhood, in order to rouse them up to seek and to merit the rewards of Heaven. He became famous for miracles, for his prayers restored sufferers from all kinds of disease and affliction. He cured some who were vexed by unclean spirits not only by laying on of hands, exhorting, and exorcising – that is by actual contact – but even from afar, merely by praying or predicting their cure, as in the case of the sheriff's wife.

Some of the monks preferred their old way of life to the rule. He overcame these by patience and forbearance, bringing them round little by little through daily example to a better frame of mind. At chapter meetings he was often worn down by bitter insults, but would put an end to the arguments simply by rising and walking out, calm and unruffled. Next day he would give the same people exactly the same admonitions, as though there had been no unpleasantness the previous day. In this way he gradually won their obedience. He was wonderfully patient and unsurpassed for courage in enduring physical or mental hardship. Though overwhelmed by sorrow at these monks' recalcitrance, he managed to keep a cheerful face. It was clear to everyone that it was the Holy Spirit within giving him strength to smile at attacks from without. Such was his zeal for prayer that sometimes he would keep vigil for three or four nights at a stretch, so they say, without ever sleeping in his bed – and there was nowhere to rest outside the dormitory. Whether he was praying alone in some secret place or saying his psalms, he always did manual work to drive away the heaviness of sleep, or else he would do the rounds of the island, kindly inquiring how everything was getting on, relieving the tedium of his long vigils and psalm-singing by walking about. He would upbraid the monks for their softness in being annoyed if any restless brother should awaken them at the wrong moment.

'Nobody vexes me,' he would say, 'by waking me up. In fact I am pleased, for by driving away my drowsiness he has made me turn my mind to doing something useful.'

So full was he of sorrow for sin, so much aflame with heavenly yearnings, that he could never finish mass without shedding tears. He would imitate, as was only fitting, the rite he was performing, by offering himself up to God with a contrite heart. He urged his people to lift up their hearts and give thanks to the Lord God more by the yearnings of his own heart than by the sound of his voice, more by sighs than by chanting. His thirst for righteousness made him quick to reprove wrong-doers, but his gentleness made him speedy to forgive penitents. Often as they were pouring out their sins he would be the first to burst into tears, tears of sympathy with their weakness, and, though he had no need, would show them how to make up for their sins by doing the penance himself. He wore quite ordinary clothes, neither remarkably neat nor noticeably slovenly. The monastery follows his example to this day. The monks are discouraged from wearing expensively dyed cloth and are expected to be content with natural wool.

By these and other similar spiritual works the venerable prior fired all good men with the desire to emulate him and recalled the wicked and the rebels against the rule from their obstinacy in error.

## CHAPTER 17

*How he banished demons from the Farne Island and built himself a dwelling-place there*

AFTER many years in the monastery he finally entered with great joy and with the goodwill of the abbot and monks into the remoter solitude he had so long sought, thirsted after, and prayed for. He was delighted that after a long and spotless active life he should be thought worthy to ascend to the stillness of divine contemplation. He rejoiced to have attained to the condition of those of whom the psalmist proclaims: 'They shall go from strength to strength; the God of gods shall be seen in Sion.' To learn the first steps of the hermit's life he retired to a more secluded place in the outer precincts of the monastery. Not till he had first gained victory over our invisible enemy by solitary prayer and fasting did he take it on himself to seek out a remote battlefield farther away from his fellow men. The Farne is an island far out to sea, unlike Lindisfarne, which is an island in the strict sense of the word only twice a day, when cut off by the tide. When the tide is out it is joined to the mainland. (The Greeks call this kind of tide '*rheuma*'.) The Farne lies a few miles to the south-east of Lindisfarne, cut off on the landward side by very deep water and facing, on the other side, out towards the limitless ocean. The island was haunted by devils; Cuthbert was the first man brave enough to live there alone. At the entry of our soldier of Christ armed with 'the helmet of salvation, the shield of faith and the sword of the spirit which is the word of God' the devil fled and his host of allies with him. Cuthbert, having routed the enemy, became monarch of the place, in token of which he built a city worthy of his power and put up houses to match. The structure was almost circular in plan, from four to five poles in diameter, and the walls on the outside were higher than a man. Out of picty he made the walls higher inside by cutting away the solid rock at the bottom, so that with only the sky to look at, eyes and thoughts might be kept from wandering and inspired to seek for higher things. This same wall he built not with cut stone or bricks and mortar but with rough stones and peat dug out of the enclosure itself. Some of these stones were so big that four men could hardly lift them, but with the help of angels he managed to fit them into the wall. There were two buildings, an oratory and one for living in. He finished off the walls inside and out by digging away a lot of the soil. The roofs were of rough-hewn timber and straw. Near the landing-place there was a bigger house for the visiting brethren to stay in, with a spring close by.

CHAPTER 18

*How his prayer brought forth water out of the dry land. His life as a hermit*

THE dwelling-place, built on almost solid rock, had no water supply. So one day he summoned the brethren – for he had not yet cut himself off from his visitors – and said :

'The place I have chosen, as you can see, is without a well. Pray with me, I beseech you, that He who "turns the solid rock into a standing water and the flint into fountains of water" may, "giving glory not unto us but to His Name", open a spring of water for us on this rocky ground. If we dig in the centre of my little enclosure I believe He will "make us drink from the river of His pleasures".'

They dug a pit and found it next morning full of water springing up from beneath. Without a doubt it was the prayers of the saint that had brought forth water from ground of the driest, hardest kind. This water, strangely enough, kept its original level, never spilling over on to the ground nor sinking as it was drawn out. God in his bounty willed that there should never be any less, nor any more, than was needed.

Once the brethren had helped him to build the place, he lived completely alone. At first, if they came over to visit him,

he would go out and see to their needs; he would, for
instance wash their feet in warm water. Sometimes they made
him take off his shoes and let them return the compliment,
for care of his own body was so far from his thoughts that he
kept his soft leather boots on his feet for months on end without ever removing them. If he put new boots on at Easter
they would not come off till the next Easter and then only
for the Washing of the Feet in church on Maundy Thursday.
The monks found long thick calluses, where the boots had
chafed his shins through all his prayers and genuflexions.

But as time went on his zeal for perfection led him to shut
himself away from sight within the hermitage, rarely talking
to visitors even from inside, and if he did so then only
through the window. Thus he learned to live a hermit's life
of prayer and fasting. He used to keep the window open and
enjoy seeing his brethren and being seen by them, but in the
end he blocked it up and opened it only to give a blessing or
for some definite need.

<br>

## CHAPTER 19

*How, at a word, he drove the birds away from the crops
he had sown with his own hands*

AT first he took bread from his visitors and water from his
own well; then he thought it would be better to follow the
example of the fathers and live by his own hands. He asked
for implements to work the land with and wheat to sow, but
though he planted in spring there was nothing ready by mid-
summer.

'It's either the nature of the ground,' he said to the brethren, 'or the will of God, but the wheat certainly is not growing. So bring barley and we shall see whether that will produce anything. If God does not see fit to give increase, then
rather than live off others I shall return to the monastery.'

The barley was brought long past the proper time for planting, when there was no hope of it growing, but it soon sprang
up and brought forth a very good crop. When it began to
ripen the birds came down and set about devouring it. (This

tale was told by the pious servant of God himself, for it was his custom, being by nature friendly and cheerful, to strengthen the belief of his colleagues by recounting some of the blessings with which his own faith had been rewarded.)

'Why are you eating crops you yourselves did not grow?' he asked the birds. 'Perhaps you have greater need of them than I. If God has given you permission, then do as He bade you; if not, be off with you, stop damaging other people's property.'

They flew off at his first word and did no further damage. These two miracles of the venerable servant of God are reminiscent of the doings of two of the fathers. In bringing water out of the rock he reminds one of a similar miracle performed by St Benedict – only he brought it forth more abundantly because there were more people in need – and in driving away the birds he was following the example of St Antony who, by words alone, restrained wild asses from trampling his little garden.

### CHAPTER 20

*How the ravens said their prayers and brought the man of God a gift to make up for the harm they had done*

This is the place to recount another of the blessed Cuthbert's miracles similar to one of our father Benedict's, in which human pride and obstinacy are openly put to shame by the humble obedience of birds. One day some ravens which had long inhabited the island were seen tearing the straw from the roof of the visitors' house and carrying it off to build their nests. The saint reproved them with a slight gesture of the right hand and told them to leave the monks' property alone. They merely scorned his command.

'In the Name of Jesus Christ, depart forthwith!' he shouted. 'Do not dare remain to do more damage.'

They flew off shamefacedly almost before he had finished speaking. Three days later one of a pair of them returned, and finding Cuthbert digging, stood before him, with feathers outspread and head bowed low to its feet in sign of grief. Using whatever signs it could to express contrition it very humbly asked pardon. When Cuthbert realized what it meant, he gave permission for them all to return. Back they came with a fitting gift – a lump of pig's lard. Cuthbert would often show this to his visitors, inviting them to grease their shoes with it.

'What care should not men take,' he would say, 'to cultivate obedience and humility when the very birds hasten to wash away their faults of pride by prayers, tears, and gifts.'

The birds stayed on the island many years to set men a good example of reform, building their nests but never presuming to do harm to anyone. Let no one think it ridiculous to learn a lesson in virtue from birds. Does not Solomon instruct us: 'Go to the ant thou sluggard, consider her ways and be wise'?

## CHAPTER 21

### *How even the sea served him*

NOT only the inhabitants of air and ocean but the sea itself, following the examples of the air and the fire cited above, showed respect for the venerable old man. No wonder; it is hardly strange that the rest of creation should obey the wishes and commands of a man who has dedicated himself with complete sincerity to the Lord's service. We, on the other hand, often lose that dominion over creation which is ours by right through neglecting to serve its Creator. The very sea, I say, was quick to lend him aid when he needed it.

He set about constructing within the walls of his dwelling a small shed which should be big enough for his day to day requirements. It was to be built towards the sea with the floor over a long deep cleft hollowed out by the constant action of the waves. It was to be twelve foot long, for that was the length of the cleft, so he asked the monks to bring him some planks of that length for floorboards the next time they came. They willingly agreed, received his blessing, went off home and forgot all about it. Back they came on the appointed day but without the wood. He gave them a very warm welcome, commending them to God with the usual prayer, then asked:

'Where is the wood?' Then they remembered. They confessed they had forgotten and asked him to pardon their negligence. The kindly old man soothed their anxiety with a gentle word and bade them stay till next morning: 'For I do not believe God will forget my wish.' They complied with his request. The following morning when they went out there was a piece of wood of the correct length thrown up by the tide right under the site of the shed. They marvelled at the sanctity of a man whom the very elements obeyed, and blushed with shame at their own slackness in needing to be reminded by inanimate nature what obedience is due to saints.

CHAPTER 22

*How he exhorted many who came to him to the ways of salvation and pointed out the weaknesses in the snares of our old enemy*

Now Cuthbert had great numbers of people coming to him not just from Lindisfarne but even from the remote parts of Britain, attracted by his reputation for miracles. They confessed their sins, confided in him about their temptations, and laid open to him the common troubles of humanity they were labouring under – all in the hope of gaining consolation from so holy a man. They were not disappointed. No one left unconsoled, no one had to carry back the burdens he came with. Spirits that were chilled with sadness he could warm back to hope again with a pious word. Those beset with worry he brought back to thoughts of the joys of Heaven. He showed them that both good fortune and bad were transitory in this world. To men beset with temptation he would skilfully disclose all the wiles of the devil, explaining that a soul lacking in love for God or man is easily caught in the devil's nets, while one that is strong in the faith can, with God's grace, brush them aside like so many spiders' webs.

'How often have the demons tried to cast me headlong from yonder rock; how often have they hurled stones as if to kill me; with one fantastic temptation after another they have sought to disillusion me into retreating from this battle-field; but they have never yet succeeded in harming either soul or body, nor do they terrify me.'

He very often stressed that the brethren ought not to marvel at his way of life, as though it were especially exalted to prefer to cast aside the cares of the world and live apart.

'It is the monastic life you ought to stand in awe of. In that life everything is subject to the abbot; the times of prayer, fasting, vigils, and work are governed by his will. I have known many abbots who for purity of mind and depth of prophetic power have far surpassed my poor self – Boisil, for example, a man to be named with all honour and veneration. He was old and I but a youth when he brought me up in the monastery at Melrose. While he was instructing me he prophesied my whole future accurately. One of those prophecies has yet to happen; would to God it might not.'

Here he referred to Boisil's prophecy that he would one day be a bishop. His desire for a more secluded life made him tremble at the thought.

## CHAPTER 23

*How Abbess Aelfflaed and one of her nuns were cured by his cincture*

CUTHBERT did not cease to perform miracles of healing even though far removed from mankind. There was a holy handmaid of Christ, Aelfflaed, who, as one of the joys of her virginal state, had charge of a great company of nuns. She looked after them with motherly love, adding to her royal rank the yet more noble adornment of a high degree of holiness. She had a deep affection for Cuthbert. She herself told the following story to that most reverend priest of the Lindisfarne church, Herefrith, who in turn told it to me.

She had been seriously ill for a long time and seemed almost on the point of dying. The doctors could do nothing for her. By God's grace she was suddenly removed from danger of death though not entirely cured; the internal pain went and she regained the use of her limbs but still could not stand upright nor move about except on all fours. She began to fear that the condition might be permanent, since she had long since given up hope of getting any help from doctors. One day oppressed by these sad thoughts her mind wandered to the peaceful life Cuthbert led.

'How I wish I had something belonging to my dear Cuthbert!' she sighed. 'As I trust and believe in God I know for certain that I should be quickly healed.'

Shortly afterwards someone arrived with a linen cincture sent by Cuthbert. She was delighted with the gift and realized that her wishes had been made known to him by heavenly means. She girded herself with it and next morning was able to stand up straight. Two days later she was completely well. A few days after this one of the nuns was seized with excruciating pains in the head. She got daily worse until it seemed unlikely she could last much longer. The venerable abbess paid her a visit, saw how ill she was, and bound up her head with the cincture. The pain left her that very same day and she was cured. She took off the cincture and hid it in her locker. When it was required by the abbess a few days later it was nowhere to be found, neither in the locker nor anywhere else. This was God's doing: by those two miracles of healing he manifested Cuthbert's holiness to the faithful, and then removed the cincture lest it should lead the faithless to doubt such sanctity. Had it been allowed to remain, the sick would have flocked to it and if anyone through lack of merit were left uncured, the fact would be taken not as a proof of that person's unworthiness but as a reason for disparaging the relic. So, as I said, by a merciful dispensation of Divine Providence, first the belief of the faithful was strengthened, and then all danger of disparagement by the envious or unbelieving was removed.

CHAPTER 24

*What he predicted about King Ecgfrith in answer to
Aelfflaed. He foretells his own consecration*

THAT same holy virgin Aelfflaed, mother of the handmaids of
Christ, sent to Cuthbert on another occasion begging him in
God's name to come and talk over some important matter. He
took a boat and sailed with his brethren to the appointed meeting place, Coquet Island, so called because it lies opposite
the mouth of the Coquet. It was renowned for its monasteries. In the course of conversation, after Cuthbert had
answered her queries at length, she suddenly broke off and
flung herself before him, adjuring him by the awful name of
the King of Heaven and His Angels to tell her how long her
brother Ecgfrith would last and who was to rule after him.

'I know you can tell me,' she said, 'if only you will, for the
spirit of prophecy is strong in you.'

Her oath frightened him, yet he still shrank from revealing
the truth.

'It surprises me,' he answered, 'that a sensible woman, and
one so well versed in the scriptures should think of calling
human life long. Does not the psalmist declare "our years are
reckoned as a spider's web"? Does not Solomon exclaim: "If
a man live many years and rejoice in them all, yet let him
remember the days of darkness, for they shall be many. When
they come the past is reckoned as vanity."? Then how much
shorter must a man's life appear when he happens to be in his
last year with death at the gates?'

She wept at such dire prophecies, then wiped her face and
with true feminine audacity adjured him by the Divine
Majesty to say who would be her brother's heir, since he had
neither children nor brothers. Cuthbert was silent for a while,
then said: 'Do not say there is no heir. One will come whom
you will embrace with as much sisterly affection as though he
were Ecgfrith's own self.'

'Then tell me where he is!' she cried.

'Look at the sea,' he replied. 'It abounds in islands. God could easily provide a ruler for the English from one of them.'

She realized he was hinting at Aldfrith, the supposed son of Ecgfrith's father, who was away in Ireland being educated. She knew also that Ecgfrith wanted to see Cuthbert a bishop and she wanted to know whether the proposal would be carried out. She began again:

'Oh how divided in aim are the hearts of men! Some enjoy the wealth they have gained, others love riches but never have any to enjoy. You spurn worldly glory when offered you and reject a bishopric – than which there is nothing higher in the sight of men – in preference to that barren fastness.'

'I know I am not worthy,' he replied, 'but I know too that the decree of the Supreme Ruler cannot be escaped, no matter where one might flee to. If however, I am forced to shoulder a burden, I do not think it will be for long. After two years, perhaps, I shall be allowed to go back to my accustomed solitude and peace. Now I command you in the Name of our Lord and Saviour not to tell anyone what I have said while I am still alive.'

He expounded many other questions for her and gave her necessary advice, then went back to the Farne to cultivate the solitary life.

Shortly afterwards there was a great synod presided over by Archbishop Theodore of happy memory, in the presence of King Ecgfrith, at which Cuthbert, by general consent, was elected Bishop of Lindisfarne. Letters and messengers were sent to him repeatedly, but he refused to move. The King himself and that most holy bishop, Trumwine, with numerous devout and influential personages sailed across, knelt down and adjured him by the Lord, and wept and pleaded with him, until at last he came forth, very tearful, from his beloved hiding-place and was taken to the synod. Very reluctantly he was overcome by their unanimous decision and compelled to submit to the yoke of the episcopacy. The consecration was postponed till the end of winter, which was just then beginning. His prophecy was completely fulfilled; next year Ecgfrith was slain by the Picts and the throne went to his bastard brother Aldfrith recently returned from his studies in

Ireland, where he had willingly exiled himself for the love of learning.

## CHAPTER 25

*How as bishop elect he cured the ailing servant of one of the king's bodyguards with holy water*

AFTER his election the man of God returned to his island and went on fighting the good fight in secret with unabated zeal. Then his holy bishop, Eata, called him to Melrose to converse with him. On the way back one of King Ecgfrith's bodyguards came to meet him and asked him to turn aside on an urgent matter, namely to confer a blessing on his house and homestead. Cuthbert arrived at the house and was most hospitably treated. One of the servants was ill.

'Thanks be to God, holy father,' said the man, 'for your kindness in coming to visit us and enter our home. Your coming will, I feel sure, be a great boon to us. Our servant is tormented with some foul disease and is in such pain today that he seems more like a dying than a sick man. His extremeties look dead already and he is only just breathing.'

Cuthbert blessed some water and gave it to Baldhelm, another servant, ordering him to give it to the sick man to drink. The third time it was poured down his throat he fell into a deep sleep – a complete contrast to his previous condition. This happened in the evening. He passed a quiet night and the following morning his master found him restored to full health. Baldhelm is still alive and now a priest of the church at Lindisfarne, an office which he adorns with every virtue. It is sweeter than honey to him to recount Cuthbert's miracles to any who care to know them; he told me this one himself.

## CHAPTER 26

*His way of life as a bishop*

THIS venerable man of God, Bishop Cuthbert, following the teaching and practice of the apostles, adorned his office with good works. He protected the flock committed to him by constant prayer on their behalf, by wholesome admonition and – which is the real way to teach – by example first and precept later. He delivered 'the poor man from him that was too strong for him, the poor and the needy from him that despoiled them'. He took care to comfort the sad and faint-hearted and to bring back those that delighted in evil to a godly sorrow. He strictly maintained his old frugality and took delight in preserving the rigours of the monastery amidst the pomp of the world. He fed the hungry, clothed the destitute, and had all the other marks of a perfect bishop. These outward signs and wonders in which he excelled give adequate proof of his virtue. It has been my task to give a brief account of some of them.

## CHAPTER 27

*How he saw in spirit, though absent from the scene, the destruction of King Ecgfrith, as he had predicted*

WHEN King Ecgfrith led his army against the Picts and devastated their lands with brutal and ferocious cruelty – an extremely rash move – then Cuthbert knew that his prophecy to Aelfflaed was nearing fulfilment. He set off therefore to Carlisle, to speak with the queen who had arranged to stay there in her sister's convent to await the outcome of the war. The day after his arrival the citizens conducted him round the city walls to see a remarkable Roman fountain that was built into them. He was suddenly disturbed in spirit. He leaned heavily on his staff, turned his face dolefully to the wall, then straightening himself and looking up to the sky he sighed deeply and said almost in a whisper: 'Perhaps at this moment the battle is being decided.'

A priest who was standing by realized what he was referring to, and burst out imprudently with : 'How do you know?'

'Do you not see how strangely disturbed the air is? Who can fathom the judgements of God?'

He hurried straight back to the queen and spoke to her in secret. 'Tomorrow being Sunday you cannot travel. Monday morning at daybreak leave in your chariot for the royal city.

Enter quickly for perhaps the king has been slain. Tomorrow I have been invited to a neighbouring monastery to dedicate the chapel, but as soon as the dedication is over I shall follow you.'

On the Sunday morning at the end of his sermon, as the congregation were expressing their approval, he took up this prophetic theme again:

'Brethren, I beseech you to watch as the apostle warns you. Stand firm in the faith, play the man, lest sudden temptation find you unprepared. Be mindful rather of the Lord's command: "Watch and pray lest ye enter into temptation."' (Now there had recently been a devastating pestilence in the area which had carried off numbers of people in a great wave of destruction. They thought he meant the plague would return.) He continued: 'One day, when I was living alone on the Farne Island, some of the monks came over to see me on Christmas Day to persuade me to leave my abode and pass so sacred and so joyful a feast in their company. I gave way to their earnest requests and came out. We sat down outside and banqueted. In the middle of the meal I said to them: "Brethren, I implore you, let us act prudently and be on our guard lest through taking neither care nor heed we be seduced by temptation."

' "For goodness' sake," they replied, "let us enjoy ourselves today – it is Christmas, the birthday of Our Lord Jesus Christ."

' "Very well, let us," I replied. As things went on and we were enjoying our dinner, feeling convivial and telling stories, I broke in again to warn them to be earnest in prayer and vigils and to be ready against all temptation.

' "Well said," they answered. "You give excellent advice but there are plenty of fast days, plenty of time for vigils and prayers. Today we are rejoicing in the Lord. This is the day the angels announced Christ's birth to the shepherds, giving them glad tidings of great joy, a joy to be celebrated by them and all mankind."

'To which I answered: "Very well, let us do so." When however, while we were still feasting and passing the day merrily, I repeated the self-same words of warning a third

time, they realized I was not anxious without good reason and
they began to be afraid:

' "Let us do as you say. It does indeed behove us to be ever
on the watch, our loins ever girt against the snares of the devil
and all temptations."

'I must confess I knew as little as they did whether some
new temptation would attack us or no, but I felt an instinctive
warning that one should be on constant guard against sudden
storms of temptation. The following morning they left for
Lindisfarne and returned to find one of their brethren dead of
the plague. The disease raged for month after month, lasted
a whole year and carried off almost that whole renowned
company of spiritual fathers and brothers. So now brethren,
persevere in prayer so that, should tribulation befall you it
will not find you unprepared.'

Because of this story they naturally thought he was warning them against the plague. Next day a fugitive from the battle arrived, whose tale of woe threw light on Cuthbert's dark
hints. The same day, nay, the very same hour that Cuthbert
received the message as he stood by the fountain, the king
and all his bodyguards had been slaughtered by the enemy.

CHAPTER 28

*How he predicted his own death to Hereberht the hermit*

SHORTLY afterwards he was invited to Carlisle to ordain
some deacons to the priesthood and to give the religious habit
with his blessing to the queen. There was a holy priest called
Hereberht, long bound to Cuthbert in spiritual friendship,
living the hermit's life on an island in that great lake from
which the River Derwent flows. He used to come to Cuthbert
every year to take counsel about his eternal salvation. Hearing
that he was staying at Carlisle, Hereberht came to him, seeking, as usual, to be fired with an ever-increasing love for the
things of Heaven. While they were regaling each other with
draughts of celestial wisdom Cuthbert said casually: 'Remember, brother Hereberht, to ask me now whatever you
need to ask. This is the last time we shall see each other with

the eyes of the flesh, for I know the time is at hand when I must lay aside my earthly tabernacle; the time of my departure is nigh.'

Hereberht flung himself at his feet and sobbed.

'In the Lord's name, do not leave me. Think of your friend and ask the Divine Mercy to grant that, as we have served Him together on earth, so we may journey forth together to see His glory in Heaven. You know I have always striven to follow your commands, and whenever ignorance or human frailty has led me astray I have always chastised myself as you judged fit.'

The bishop prayed fervently and was immediately given to know that his prayer was answered.

'Rise up, brother; do not weep. Rejoice and be glad, for the Divine Mercy has granted our prayer.'

This was borne out by the course of events. Hereberht departed, and they saw each other on earth no more, but their souls left their bodies at one and the same moment and were soon carried to the celestial kingdom by an angel host, to be united with each other in the beatific vision. Hereberht's death was preceded by a long racking illness, inflicted perhaps by God in His mercy, to make sure that, if previously he had lagged behind Cuthbert in merit, he might now be made equal to his intercessor through suffering and so deserve to depart this life with him at the same time and be received into the same eternal bliss.

## CHAPTER 29

### *He sends a priest with holy water to the wife of a bodyguard of the king*

ONE day, as he was going round the diocese giving saving counsel in all the houses and hamlets of the countryside, and laying his hand on the newly baptized so that the grace of the Holy Spirit might come down upon them, he came to the house of a member of the royal bodyguard whose wife lay ill and seemed to be dying. The man ran to meet him, knelt down and thanked God that he had come, brought him into the house, and made him most welcome. After the formal hospitality of having his hands and feet washed, the bishop sat down. Then the man told him that his wife was desperately ill and begged him to bless some holy water to sprinkle on her.

'I am sure,' he said, 'God will grant her a speedy recovery, or if she must die, put an end to her long agony and take her without delay.'

Cuthbert had water brought, blessed it, and gave it to a priest to sprinkle over the sick woman. The priest entered her bedroom and found her lying there looking like a corpse. He sprinkled the bed, sprinkled her, opened her mouth, and poured a little of the life-giving draught down her throat. The patient was quite unaware of what was being done, but as soon as the water touched her an astonishing thing happened: she was immediately restored to full health both of body and mind. She came to, blessed and thanked the Lord for deigning to send such guests to cure her, and then, rising from her bed, ministered to those who had ministered to her, the patient tending the physicians. What a pleasant sight to see that of all the members of so noble a household the lady of the house herself was the first to offer a drink to her guest, a guest whose blessing had just then removed the chalice of death from her own lips ! She followed the example of Peter's mother-in-law who, as soon as Christ had cured her of the fever, 'forthwith rose and ministered unto Him and His disciples'.

### CHAPTER 30

*He cures a girl of pains in the head and side by anointing her with oil*

HERE is another miracle similar to the last and testified to by many eyewitnesses, among whom there is the holy priest Aethilwald, one of Cuthbert's retinue at the time and now abbot of Melrose.

Cuthbert was making his usual preaching mission through the villages and had come to one where there were a few nuns. They had fled from their own monastery for fear of the barbarian army shortly before, and had been lodged in the village by Cuthbert. One of them, a relation of Aethilwald, was seriously ill, seized with pains in the head and all down one side, so that the doctors had given her up. Cuthbert's companions pointed this out to him and begged him to heal her. Full of pity for her wretchedness he anointed her with holy oil. She began to improve from that very moment and in a few days completely recovered.

### CHAPTER 31

*How a sick man was healed with bread blessed by Cuthbert*

IT would hardly be right to omit to mention a miracle performed by the power of that same venerable man but without his being actually present. You have already heard of the Hildmer sheriff – it was his wife Cuthbert exorcized. Hildmer himself was later confined to bed with a dangerous illness and grew daily worse till it seemed he could hardly last another minute. His friends had crowded round the bed to console him, when one of them suddenly remembered that he had in his pocket a piece of bread which Cuthbert had shortly beforehand blessed and given him.

'I am sure this will restore him to health,' he said, 'unless our slowness to believe prevents it.'

They were all laymen but very devout, and having discussed the matter each one said he had not the least doubt that Hildmer could be healed by partaking of the bread. They filled a cup with water, dropped a tiny piece of bread in, and gave it him to drink. The moment the water the bread had made holy entered his stomach all internal pain left him and his body ceased to atrophy. Once the pain was gone, health and strength returned, inciting him and all who saw or heard of the unexpected recovery to praise Cuthbert's holiness and marvel at the strength and sincerity of Hildmer's faith.

CHAPTER 32

*How, on a journey, he restored to life a youth who was
brought to him dying*

ONCE when this most holy shepherd of the Lord's flock was
doing the round of his sheepfolds, he came into a rough
mountain area whither many had gathered from the scattered
villages to be confirmed. Now there was no church nor even a
place in the mountains fit to receive a bishop and his retinue,
so the people put up tents for him while for themselves
they made huts of felled branches as best they could. Cuthbert
preached twice to the milling crowds and brought down the
grace of the Holy Ghost by imposition of hands on those
newly regenerated in Christ. In the middle of the ceremonies
some women appeared bringing in on a litter a youth all
wasted away by a long nagging disease. They laid him down
at the edge of the wood and sent to Cuthbert to ask permission
to bring him forward for a blessing. When the youth had
been brought in Cuthbert saw how gravely ill he was and
bade everyone move farther off. He had recourse to his usual
armoury, prayer, gave a blessing and drove away the disease
for which the doctors, despite their skill in concocting medi-
cines, had been unable to devise a cure. The youth regained
his strength, stood up and gave thanks to God, and went back
home with the women who had brought him. And so it came
to pass that he who had been carried in prostrate by sorrow-
ing women walked home hale and hearty amid their rejoicings.

CHAPTER 33

*How, when the plague was on, he restored a dying boy to
his mother*

AT this same time the plague broke out and dealt such havoc
that of great villages and estates once crowded with inhabitants only a tiny scattered remnant remained, and sometimes
not even that. Our most holy father Cuthbert went round the

diocese with unflagging zeal, preaching and bringing much-needed consolation to the few people left. In one village he exhorted everyone he found and said to the priest, 'Do you suppose there is anyone else left in the place who needs visiting and speaking to, or can I now move on to the next?'

The priest looked all round and pointed out a woman some distance away, who had just before lost one son and was now holding another, dying, in her arms. Her tear-stained face gave ample proof of both past and present ills. Cuthbert went up to her without delay, blessed the boy, and kissed him.

'Have no fear,' he said to the mother. 'Do not grieve. The child will get better and live, and you will lose no more of your family.'

Mother and child both lived long afterwards, thus proving the prophecy true.

## CHAPTER 34

*How he beheld being carried heavenwards the soul of a man who had been killed in a fall from a tree*

CUTHBERT knew that he was soon to die and made up his mind accordingly to lay aside the burden of pastoral office and retire to a life of solitude. Once free from material worries he might be able to give himself undividedly to his prayers and psalms, to prepare himself for death or, rather, eternal life. But he wished to make a visitation of the diocese first and visit the homes of some other of the faithful in the neighbourhood to exhort them and give them the strength they needed. Then he would withdraw to the joy and refreshment of his longed-for solitude. As he was going the rounds, that most noble and holy virgin Aelfflaed, of whom we have spoken above, asked him to come to see her at one of the estates belonging to her monastery in order to converse with her and consecrate a church. There were a good number of people, servants of God, living on this estate. When they had sat down to dinner, Cuthbert suddenly turned his attention from the worldly feast to meditate on spiritual things. His limbs went limp and useless, his face changed colour, his eyes became fixed in amazement, and the knife fell from his hand to the table. The priest, his minister, who was standing near, lent over to the abbess and whispered: 'Ask the bishop what he sees, for his hand did not tremble and let go the knife without reason. He is having some kind of vision which is denied us.'

She turned to him at once.

'My lord bishop, I beg you to tell me what you have just seen – your hand did not slacken and let the knife fall for no reason at all.'

He tried to conceal the fact that he had seen anything extraordinary by merely laughing it off:

'Well, I cannot eat all day. I must pause sometime.'

But she pestered him into telling.

'I saw,' he admitted, 'the soul of some holy man being borne by the hands of angels into the joy of Heaven.'

'Where did he come from?'

'From your monastery.'

She wanted to know his name.

'You yourself will tell me tomorrow in the middle of mass.'

She sent off at once to the main monastery to see whose soul had been so recently snatched from his body, but the messenger found them all safe and sound and set off back the next morning. On the way he came across a group of men bearing the body of one of their brothers on a cart to burial. He learnt, on asking, that it was one of the shepherds, a good-living man, who had climbed a tree too recklessly and had fallen. His injuries proved mortal and he had passed away at the very time Cuthbert saw him carried heavenwards. On being informed Aelfflaed hastened to the bishop, then in the middle of the dedication ceremonies, and, woman-like, acted as though stupefied, announcing, as if it were fresh news: 'My lord bishop, remember at mass my servant Hadwald who died yesterday of a fall from a tree.'

Then everyone saw, as clear as could be, the extent and scope of Cuthbert's prophetic gifts – not only could he see a soul being carried heavenwards at the very moment of death but also foresee what others would tell him about it later.

## CHAPTER 35

*How he gave water the flavour of wine simply by tasting it*

WHEN he had gone through the upper districts of the diocese in order, he came to a convent of virgins close to the mouth of the Tyne, a place we have already mentioned. Abbess Verca, a devout and, in the eyes of the world, a noble woman, gave him a magnificent welcome. When the after-dinner rest was over Cuthbert said he felt thirsty and would like a drink. They asked whether he wanted wine or beer.

'Give me water,' came the reply.

It was drawn from the well and brought. He blessed it, drank a little, and gave it to his priest, who gave it to the man who had brought it, a priest of the monastery. He asked if he might drink from the cup which the bishop had just used.

'Of course. Why not?' Cuthbert answered.

The priest drank, and it seemed to him that the water had taken on the taste of wine. Eager to have witnesses of so great a miracle he handed the cup to a brother standing by. He drank and thought he had wine in his mouth, not water. They gaped at each other in astonishment and afterwards, when they had a chance to talk, confessed that they had never tasted better wine. One of them later came to stay in our monastery at Monkwearmouth, lived with us a long time, and was peacefully buried there. I had the story from him.

## CHAPTER 36

*How certain brethren who had disobeyed him were held back by a storm at sea*

IN the second year of his episcopate Cuthbert knew that his end was nigh. He laid aside his pastoral duties and went back as soon as possible to his beloved life of solitary conflict, to give the flame of compunction time to burn away the deeply fixed thorns of worldly cares. Nevertheless he would often leave his dwelling to meet and talk to the brethren who came over to visit him.

Perhaps it would not be out of place at this juncture to insert an account of a miracle he worked about this time, to show you quite clearly that saints are to be obeyed in even their most casual commands. Here it is then :

One day some of the monks came over and Cuthbert went out to give them a few words of encouragement. He finished thus : 'Now it is time to go back to my cell. You are ready to go too, but before you set off have something to eat. Take that goose hanging up on the wall, cook it and eat it, and then set sail in the Name of the Lord.'

He blessed them and went in. They ate as he had bidden them, but, since they had plenty of their own food with them, they could not be bothered to prepare the goose. When the meal was over they made to go aboard, but a fierce storm arose making it impossible to row, with the result that they were shut in on the island for a whole week with the seas raging round them, quite unaware of the fault for which they were kept imprisoned. They sought out Cuthbert and anxiously complained about the delay. He merely preached patience, but the seventh day very graciously came out to speak to them, thinking that a word of sympathy might soothe their pain. He entered the visitors' house and, seeing the bird still hanging there uncooked, calmly upbraided them for their disobedience – he was, in fact, rather pleased.

'What ! Is that bird still hanging there uncooked ? Do you wonder the sea will not let you go ? Quickly now, put it in the pot, cook it and eat it, then the sea will calm down and you will be able to leave.'

They obeyed at once and, wondrous to relate, just as the goose began to boil in the pot, the wind died away and the waves lost their fury. They finished eating the goose, saw that the sea was smooth, and set off, arriving home with the wind behind them, overjoyed and not a little ashamed. They blush-ed at the thought of their disobedience and at their dimwitted-ness, which despite the chastisements of the Creator had kept them from realizing and correcting their fault. They rejoiced to see that God had such regard for His faithful servant that He would call up the elements to punish those who failed to respect him, and rejoiced also that He cared for them to the extent of performing a miracle to correct their errors.

This story did not come to me from any casual source but from one of that very party, the venerable monk and priest Cynimund. He is still alive and renowned far and wide for his great holiness and great age.

CHAPTER 37

*The temptations he suffered while ill and the instructions he gave about his burial just before he died*

As soon as Christmas was over Cuthbert sought out his island home once more. A crowd of the brethren gathered to see him off, one of whom, an old monk, strong in the faith though wasted away through dysentery, said to him, 'Tell us, my lord, when we may expect to see you again.'

The answer came back as plain as the question (for Cuthbert knew it was true): 'When you bring back my corpse.'

He was given almost two months to rediscover the delights of the quiet life and to fit mind and body into the strict discipline of his old routine; then he was suddenly felled by disease, to be prepared by the fires of internal pain for the joys of everlasting bliss. Let me tell you of his death verbatim, just as I had it from Herefrith, a sincerely devout priest and present abbot of Lindisfarne:

'After being wracked by three weeks of continual illness, he met his end in the following way. He took ill, you know, on a Wednesday, and it was on a Wednesday too that the disease conquered and he went to his Lord. I arrived the morning the sickness began – I had already been there three days previously with the brethren to get his blessing and words of consolation – and now gave the usual signal to let him know I had arrived. He came to the window, but when I greeted him he could only sigh.

' "What is wrong, my lord? Have you had an attack during the night?"

' "Yes," he said, "it came last night."

'I thought he was referring to his old complaint that used to trouble him nearly every day, not to anything new. Without further question I asked for his blessing as it was time to be rowing back.

' "Do as you intend," he said. "Board your vessel and go safely home. When God takes my soul, bury me here close to the oratory, on the south side and to the east of that holy cross I myself put up. To the north of the oratory you will find a stone coffin hidden under the turf, a present from the holy Abbot Cudda. Put my body in it, wrapped in the cloth you will find there. Abbess Verca gave it me as a present but I was loath to wear it. Out of affection for her I carefully put it aside to use as a winding-sheet."

'Hearing this I exclaimed : "Father, now that you yourself have told me you are dying, I beg you to let some of the brethren stay and look after you."

' "Go now and come back at the proper time."

'I insisted that there should be someone by him but he would not agree. Finally I asked when we were to come back.

' "When God wants. He will show you."

'We carried out his directions. Calling together the brethren in church I ordered constant prayer on his behalf, telling them that I gathered from his words that he would soon be with the Lord. I was anxious to return, but a storm kept us back for five days ; events were later to prove that this was the work of Providence. Almighty God, in order that his servant might be purified from every trace of human frailty and to show his adversaries their impotence against his strength of faith, willed him to be cut off from mankind for so long to test him by physical suffering and by exposing him to still fiercer conflict with our ancient enemy. When the storm abated we reached the island to find that he had left his cell and was sitting in the house where we used to lodge. The other monks had to go over to the shore on some necessary errand but I stayed and lost no time in seeing to his needs. One of his feet needed attention ; it had been swollen for a long time and had now developed an ulcer and was suppurating. I heated some water and bathed it. I then gave him some warm wine and tried to make him taste it. You could see from his face that what with the illness and lack of food besides his strength was all drained away. When I had finished he sat down quietly on the couch and I sat beside him. He was silent, so I began the conversation.

' "My lord bishop, I can see how much you have suffered since we left you, and I wonder why you would not allow anyone to stay to look after you."

' "It was God's will that I should be left to suffer awhile without help or company. From the time you left the sickness grew steadily worse; and I got up and came out here so that when you did arrive to take care of me, you would be able to find me without having to bother to enter the monastery. From the time I came in here and settled myself down I have not moved a limb but have remained in the same position these five days and nights."

' "But my lord, how can you live like this? Have you gone without food all this time?"

'He turned back the coverlet on which he sat and showed me five onions.

' "This has been my food for the last five days. Whenever my mouth was parched or burned with excessive hunger or thirst I refreshed and cooled myself with these."

'One of the onions was less than half nibbled away. He added: "My assailants have never tempted me so sorely as they have during the past five days."

'I did not dare inquire what kind of temptations they were but contented myself with asking him to let himself be waited upon. He consented and let some of us stay, one of whom was the priest Bede, his personal servant. (It was his position as servant that enabled Bede to know all the presents that Cuthbert had ever received.) Cuthbert wanted him at hand in case he had forgotten to make due return for any of the gifts he had received; if that was so, Bede could remind him and give him time to return the kindness before he died. He especially asked to have another brother by him as a servant. This other monk had suffered for a long time from severe diarrhoea and could not be cured. His piety, prudence, and seriousness marked him out as a worthy witness of the saint's last words and of the way he died. I returned and told the brethren that our venerable father had ordered that he was to be buried on the island.

' "But it seems far more fitting to me," I added, "to ask him to let us bring his body back here to be given a more decent burial with proper honours in the church."

'They agreed and we went to Cuthbert.

' "We do not think lightly of your command, my lord, to be interred here, but it seemed right that we should ask for the honour of bringing your body back to the monastery to remain with us."

' "But it is my desire to rest here where I have fought my fight for the Lord and where I want to finish the course and whence I hope to be raised up by my just judge to receive the crown of righteousness. What is more, it would be less trouble for you if I did stay here, because of the influx of fugitives and every other kind of malefactor which will otherwise result. They will flee for refuge to my body, for, whatever I might be, my fame as a servant of God has been noised abroad. You will be constrained to intercede very often with the powers of this world on behalf of such men. The presence of my remains will prove extremely irksome."

'We pleaded with him a long time, insisting that all this would seem light to us through being a labour of love. At last he gave us this advice.

' "If you feel you must go against my plans and take me back there, I think it would be best to make a tomb in the interior of the basilica – then you will be able to visit it yourselves whenever you wish and also to decide who else from outside may do so."

'We thanked him on bended knee for his permission and advice and went back home. After that we paid him frequent and regular visits.

## CHAPTER 38
*How, though sick himself, he healed his servant of diarrhoea*

'He grew progressively worse and, realizing that the time of departure was at hand, gave instructions at about the third hour of the day to be carried back to his oratory and little house. We carried him back as he was too weak to walk. When we reached the door we asked him to let one of us go in with him to see to his needs. It was years since anyone but himself had gone beyond that door. He looked around at us all, caught sight of the monk who suffered from diarrhoea – whom I mentioned before – and said : "Let Wahlstod come in with me."

'Wahlstod stayed inside till about the ninth hour, then came out and called me.

' "The bishop commands you to enter. I have some marvellous news for you : from the moment I touched him as I led him into the oratory, I felt my old complaint go. Doubtless this is the action of Heaven's grace, that he who had previously healed so many when strong and well himself should now be able to cure me when he is at death's door. This is a clear sign that bodily weakness is powerless to impair the spiritual force of this holy man."

'This miracle reminds one very forcibly of a cure worked by

our venerable and holy father, Bishop Aurelius Augustinus. When
he was on his death-bed someone came with a sick man, asking
only that the bishop should lay a hand on him and he would be
healed. He answered that if he had any such powers he would
have first used them on himself. But the man pressed him, saying he had been ordered to come – he had heard in a dream
a voice saying: "Go to Bishop Augustinus and he shall cure you
with a touch of the hand." At this the bishop placed his hand on
the man to bless him and sent him home cured.

### CHAPTER 39

*His last commands to the brethren and how, having received
the viaticum, he yielded up his spirit in prayer*

'I went in to him,' Herefrith continued, 'about the ninth hour
and found him lying in a corner of the oratory opposite the altar.
I sat down beside him. He said very little, for the weight of
affliction made it hard for him to speak. But when I asked him
rather urgently what counsel he was going to leave us as his testament or last farewell, he launched into a brief but significant
discourse on peace and humility, and exhorted us to be on our
guard against those who, far from delighting in these virtues,
actively foster pride and discord :

' "Preserve amongst yourselves unfailing divine charity, and
when you have to hold council about your common affairs let
your principal aim be to reach a unanimous decision. Live in
mutual concord with all other servants of Christ ; do not despise
those of the household of the faith who come to you seeking hospitality. Receive them, put them up, and set them on their way
with kindness, treating them as one of yourselves. Do not think
yourselves any better than the rest of your companions who share
the same faith and follow the monastic life. With those who
have wandered from the unity of the Catholic faith, either through
not celebrating Easter at the proper time or through evil living,
you are to have no dealings. Never forget that if you should ever
be forced to make the choice of two evils I would much rather
you left the island, taking my bones with you, than that you
should be a party to wickedness on any pretext whatsoever, bending your necks to the yoke of schism. Strive most diligently to
learn the catholic statutes of the fathers and put them into practice. Make it your special care to carry out those rules of the
monastic life which God in His divine mercy has seen fit to give

you through my ministry. I know that, though some might think my life despicable, none the less after my death you will see that my teachings are not to be easily dismissed."

'These and like sayings he uttered at intervals, because the gravity of the disease, as I said before, had weakened his speech. He passed the day quietly till evening, awaiting the joys of the world to come, and went on peacefully with his prayers throughout the night. At the usual time for night prayer I gave him the sacraments that lead to eternal life. Thus fortified with the Lord's Body and Blood in preparation for the death he knew was now at hand, he raised his eyes heavenwards, stretched out his arms aloft, and with his mind rapt in the praise of the Lord sent forth his spirit to the bliss of Paradise.

## CHAPTER 40

*How, in accordance with the prophecy contained in the psalm they sang as he died, the monks of Lindisfarne were attacked, but, with the Lord's help, kept safe*

'I WENT out at once and announced his death to the brethren, who were themselves spending the night in prayer and vigil. As chance would have it they had reached Psalm Fifty-nine in lauds, the one beginning: "O God Thou hast cast us off and hast broken us down; Thou hast been angry and hast had compassion on us." One of the monks went without delay and lit two candles and went up, with one in each hand, to a piece of high ground to let the Lindisfarne brethren know that Cuthbert's holy soul had gone to the Lord. They had decided among themselves that this should be the sign of his holy death. The brother in the watch-tower at Lindisfarne, who was sitting up all night awaiting the news, ran quickly to the church where the monks were assembled for the night office, and as he entered they too were singing that same Psalm Fifty-nine. This, as events were to prove, was providential. For after Cuthbert was buried such a storm of trouble broke out that several monks chose to depart rather than bear the brunt of such danger.

'A year later Eadberht succeeded to the bishopric. He was a man of outstanding virtues, completely dedicated to works of charity, and a fine scripture scholar. It was with his accession that the trouble and disturbances were quelled. "The Lord," as the scriptures tell us, "did build up Jerusalem" – that is, the vision of peace – "and gather together the outcast of Israel. He healed the broken-hearted and bound up their wounds." Then the import of the psalm they had been singing when news of Cuthbert's death arrived was made plain – his fellow-citizens of the monastery might be cast down and forced out, but when the blaze of wrath had spent itself they would be brought to life again through the divine mercy. Anyone who glances at the psalm will see that the rest of the verses convey the same meaning.

'We placed the body of our venerable father in the boat and bore it across to Lindisfarne, where it was received by choirs of singers and a great crowd that had turned out to meet it. It was buried in a stone coffin on the right-hand side of the altar in the church of the Blessed Apostle Peter.'

## CHAPTER 41

*How a lotion made from the soil on to which the water used to wash Cuthbert's body had been poured was used to cure a demoniac boy*

CUTHBERT's miracles of healing did not cease with his death and burial. There was a boy on Lindisfarne possessed by a most brutal spirit. His wits were gone completely, he yelled, howled like a beast, and bit to shreds everything within reach, including his own limbs. A priest whose exorcisms had usually succeeded in putting evil spirits to flight was sent for from the monastery, but he could do nothing with this one. He advised the boy's father to strap him to a cart and bring him to the monastery to be prayed for at the relics of the martyrs. The father did as advised but the martyrs refused to grant the cure – in order to show just how high a place Cuthbert held amongst them. The lunatic boy struck terror into all who saw or heard him by his howls and groans and gnashing of teeth. No one could think of any remedy at all till suddenly one of the priests, instructed in spirit that Cuthbert could restore him to health, went secretly to the place where he knew the water from washing the corpse had been thrown out. He mixed a particle of the earth with water and poured it into the sufferer's mouth. His mouth was gaping wide, a disgusting sight, and he was yelling hideous pitiful cries, but as soon as the water touched him the cries died down, his mouth shut, the glaring bloodshot eyes closed, and his head and whole body sank into repose. He slept well and awoke next morning both from sleep and from madness to realize that he had been freed from the spirit which had beset him through the prayers and merits of Cuthbert.

Everyone was as delighted as they were astonished at the sight of the lad going round the holy places with his father, sound of mind and giving thanks to the saints for their help, while only the day before he had had no idea who or where he was. On his knees before the martyrs' relics, with the whole community standing by and joining their thanks to his, he praised God for releasing him from the scourge of the enemy. He returned home with his faith strengthened. The pit into which the water had been thrown is on view to this day. It is square, with a wooden frame round the sides, and is filled in with stones. It stands near the church where Cuthbert is buried, on the south side. From then on God granted many miracles of healing by means of those same stones and earth.

## CHAPTER 42

*How his body was found incorrupted eleven years later*

THE sublimity of the saint's earthly life was well attested by his numerous miracles. Almighty God in His Providence now chose to give further proof of Cuthbert's glory in Heaven by putting it into the minds of the brethren to dig up his bones. They expected to find the bones quite bare (as is usual with the dead), the rest of the body having dwindled away to dust. They were going to put them in a light casket in some fitting place above ground in order to give them their due veneration. Bishop Eadberht was informed of their decision sometime in mid-Lent and expressed his agreement, ordering them to carry out the ceremony on the 20th of March, the anniversary of the burial. This they did. On opening the coffin they found the body completely intact, looking as though still alive, and the joints of the limbs still flexible. It seemed not dead but sleeping. The vestments, all of them, were not merely unfaded but crisp and fresh like new, and wonderfully bright. The monks were filled with great fear and trembling; they could not speak, did not dare to look at the miracle, and hardly knew where to turn. Taking some of the outer garments with them as a sign of the incorruption – for they were afraid to touch anything that had been next to his skin – they hurried off to the bishop, who was then staying alone in a place some distance from the monastery, a place cut off by the sea at high tide. He used to spend Lent here and the forty days before Christmas in prayer and severe fasting, shedding tears of devotion. It was the place where Cuthbert had fought his solitary battle for the Lord for a while before going to the Farne. Eadberht received the vestments with joy and gladly listened to the story of the miracle, kissing the clothes with great affection, as though they had been still round the body.

'Put new vestments on the body,' he said, 'in place of those you have removed and replace the corpse in the chest you have made ready for it. For I can assure you that the spot that has been consecrated by so great a proof of heavenly virtue will not be empty for long. And blessed is he indeed to whom the Lord, the fount and author of true happiness, will grant a place of rest therein.'

He expressed his wonder in the following words (which I myself once put into verse):

'What tongue can talk calmly about the gifts of God? What eye has ever seen the joys of Paradise? That will only be possible when we leave behind our earthly bodies and are received into the arc of Heaven by the Lord Himself. See how He now honours the form of an earthly body in token of far greater glories to come! You have caused power to flow from these dear bones of Cuthbert, Lord, filling the Church with the very atmosphere of Paradise. You have bidden decay hold, as you did when you brought forth Jonah into the light of day after three days in the whale's belly. The tribe of Israel, which Pharaoh made to wander forty long years in the desert, you called to be your own people; you preserved Shadrach, Meshach and Abednego in the flames of the fiery furnace and, when earth shall tremble at the last trump, you shall raise us to glory for your Son's sake.'

When the bishop had finished this paean with great emotion and faltering speech, the brethren went off to carry out his orders. The body was wrapped in a new garment, enclosed in a light coffin, and placed on the floor of the sanctuary.

## CHAPTER 43

*Eadberht is buried in Cuthbert's tomb beneath a sarcophagus containing Cuthbert's remains*

MEANWHILE Eadberht was stricken with a painful disease. It grew daily more intense and within a short while he died, on the 6th of May to be exact. His wish, to die not suddenly but through long and wearing illness, had been granted. He was put in Cuthbert's tomb under the chest containing the incorrupted body.

Even to this day there is no lack of signs and wonders; the very clothes worn by the saint, both in life and in death, have still the power to heal.

## CHAPTER 44

*A sick man is cured by praying at the tomb*

ONE of the clergy of the reverend and holy Willibrord, Clement, bishop of the Frisians, came from abroad and stayed for a few days as a guest at Lindisfarne. Suddenly he fell gravely ill; his condition gradually worsened and was finally pronounced desperate. So severe was the pain that life and death seemed equally intolerable. Then he had an inspiration.

'Take me, I beg you,' he said to his servant, one Sunday, 'to honour Cuthbert's most holy body; for I hope to be delivered from my agony by his intercession, either by being restored to this present life or carried off to the life to come.'

The servant obeyed and – no mean task – led him hobbling along on a stick into the church. Kneeling down at the sepulchre of our most holy father and God's beloved he bowed his head to the ground and prayed for recovery. Immediately he felt such strength flow into him from the saint's incorrupt body that he rose to his feet without the least effort and walked back to his rooms without the aid of servant or staff. A few days later when he was fully himself again he set off on his intended journey.

CHAPTER 45

*How his shoes healed a paralytic*

THERE was a youth in a near-by monastery who had lost the use of all his limbs through that disease which the Greeks call paralysis. His abbot knew that the Lindisfarne monastery housed some extremely skilful physicians, so he sent him there with the request that they should do everything within their power to cure him. In compliance with the abbot's and their own bishop's command they applied every ounce of skill and knowledge they possessed, but all to no effect. The disease advanced from day to day and he became so helpless that in the end he could only open his mouth. His doctors, having so long exerted all their human skill in vain, gave up hope. Lying there despaired of, he had recourse to the Divine Physician, to Him who when sought with sincerity of heart 'pardoneth all our iniquities and healeth all our infirmities'. He asked his servant to bring him a piece of the incorruptible garments from the sacred body, believing that God, by virtue of the relic, would grant the grace of recovery. On the abbot's advice the servant brought the shoes which Cuthbert had worn in the tomb and put them on the lifeless feet of the invalid, for the paralysis had first taken hold in the feet. This was done at sunset when it was time to rest. The invalid immediately fell into a calm sleep. Suddenly, as the hours were drawing on into the silence of the night, first one foot, then the other began to twitch. The servants who were watching over him saw this quite clearly and realized that the power of the saint's relics was at work, travelling upwards through the rest of the body from the soles of the feet. The bell for the night office woke him and he sat up. He knew at once that he was cured – the muscles and all the joints of his limbs felt strong and solid and the pain had gone. He rose and stood all through matins giving thanks to God. In the morning he went to the church, and with the whole community looking on and congratulating him he went round the holy places, praying and offering the sacrifice of praise to his Saviour. There now occurred a most delightful reversal of procedure. He had been carried to Lindisfarne on a cart, completely paralysed; he walked away safe and sound with every member strong and under perfect control.

Let us not forget that this was the work of the unchanging might of God's right hand; His wonders, memorable from of old, cease not to be poured forth in brightness on the world.

CHAPTER 46

*How Felgild the hermit was cured of a swelling in the face by some of the covering of Cuthbert's cell wall*

ONE ought not to pass over a heavenly miracle granted by the Divine Mercy through part of the fabric of that holy oratory wherein our venerable father did solitary battle for the Lord. He who judges the hearts of men alone knows whether it ought to be ascribed to the merits of Cuthbert himself or to his successor Aethilwald, a man equally devoted to God. There is no reason for not believing that they both had a hand in it, together with the faith of that reverend father, Felgild, through whom and in whom the cure itself was wrought. He was the third heir to Cuthbert's spiritual battleground and is now over seventy, awaiting the end of this life and longing for the life to come. After Cuthbert's death Aethilwald came to the Farne, having been already tested many years in the monastic life until he had reached, step by step, the sublime life of a hermit.

The walls of the oratory were crumbling with age. The planks they were made of had been badly put together and had consequently come apart, leaving the place wide open to the stormy winds. Our venerable Cuthbert, more concerned with the splendours of his heavenly than his earthly abode, had simply stuffed the cracks with mud or straw or whatever else he could lay hands on, to avoid having the fervour of his prayer cooled by daily blast and downpour. When Aethilwald saw the state of the building he asked the brethren who used to flock to him to bring calf-skin. This he hoisted up as a shield against the violence of the blasts, at the corner where he, like Cuthbert before him, had most often stood or knelt in prayer. There he remained twelve years without a break until he entered the joys of Paradise. Felgild came next, and it was then that the right reverend Bishop of Lindisfarne, Eadfrith, decided to restore the oratory from its foundations up, since by then it was falling to pieces. When the work was finished Felgild had many requests from devout people for some small relic of Cuthbert or Aethilwald. The idea came to him of cutting the calf-skin into pieces, but he thought he would first try it out on himself before giving it to anyone else. His face was disfigured with a red patch and a swelling, the beginnings of which had been obvious long ago to his colleagues with whom he had lived the common life. Greater abstinence and comparative neglect of the body during his life as a hermit, coupled with the fact that he shut himself up for long periods out of the warmth of the sun and the fresh air, had made the disfigurement much worse. His face was now one mass of inflammation. Fearing that the gravity of his complaint would force him to retire from the solitary life back to the monastery, he was bold enough to pin his faith on a cure, hoping that they whose abode he delighted to dwell in would make him whole again. He put a piece of the leather in water and bathed his face with it. At once the swelling and foul scab disappeared.

The first person to tell me this was a good priest of this monastery at Jarrow. He said he saw Felgild's face when swollen and disfigured and had put his hand through the window to feel it when it was cleansed. Felgild told the story later himself, saying that everything had happened just as the priest said, and that, though he lived in confinement for as many years again, the swelling never returned. Such is the grace of that almighty God whose property is to cure many even in this world, and to heal all infirmity of body and mind in the world to come, satisfying our desires with good things and crowning us forever 'with loving-kindness and tender mercies'.

Here ends the book of the life and miracles
of St Cuthbert, Bishop of Lindisfarne

# Eddius Stephanus: Life of Wilfrid

# PREFACE

In the name of Lord Jesus Christ. Here begins the humble preface of Stephen the priest to his account of the life of St Wilfrid, a bishop worthy before God. I have no choice but to give way, my honourable masters Bishop Acca and Abbot Tatberht, before the weight of your demands and the will of the whole community – but would that I might be able to accomplish all I should like! The work is difficult, my intelligence and command of rhetoric small; none the less, though the result might come below expectation, the effort will at least pay my debt of obedience. The greatest proof of my respect for you lies in my willingness to satisfy your request even though it demands more than I have to offer. If I produce anything to justify your choice you must impute it to the grace of God. Relying on the faith and encouragement of you at whose request I begin, I have no doubts about my ultimate success. Everyone realizes that the task you have set me is one you think even myself capable of carrying out. Great profit accrues from the work itself – that of preserving the memory of Bishop Wilfrid, for simply to know what kind of man he was is in itself a sure way to virtue. In short, you can accept everything that popular report claims for him but realize that even then you know only very little about matters of great import, for believe me, nobody can possibly have the full story.

I beseech you therefore, readers, credit my report. Take no notice of the thousand envious pricks of our old enemy the devil, but give ear and assent to what I now eloquently put forth. Fortitude always meets with enmity – 'Lightning strikes the peaks first'. Do not imagine I have been so rash and presumptuous as to put down anything which would not be passed as genuine by trustworthy witnesses. I prefer silence to falsehood.

## CHAPTER I

*Stephen's preface concluded. The birth of Wilfrid and
the portent thereof*

I SHALL now embark, with the help of God, on the holy
life and merits of blessed Bishop Wilfrid, whom the Lord, in
the words of that outstanding teacher St Paul, 'foreknew,
predestined, called, justified, and glorified'. A sign from God
proved that he was sanctified while still in the womb of his
most pious mother, just as clearly as when the voice announced to Jeremiah: 'Before I formed thee in the belly I
knew thee: and before thou camest out of the womb I sanctified thee and I ordained thee a prophet unto the nations.'
His mother was in confinement, worn out with the pains of
labour, her women round her, when a group of men standing
outside saw the house suddenly take fire and flames shoot
sky high. Everyone started dashing panic-stricken in all directions, trying to douse the flames with water and rescue the
inhabitants. But the women of the house came to the door
and told them to keep calm: 'Control yourselves; a child has
been born into the world.' At first they were amazed; then
saw in what had taken place a great work of God, just as
when Moses saw the burning bush with the flames crackling yet consuming nothing. Very often, brethren, we hear
of the Holy Spirit appearing in the form of fire, for God is
a fire consuming sinners and enlightening the righteous. This
light God has ordered to be placed on a candlestick, not
hidden under a bushel, and through our holy bishop it has
shone openly on almost every church in Britain. This, the
meaning of the omen, was entirely borne out by future events.

## CHAPTER 2

*The first miracle. He chooses God in boyhood*

FROM his boyhood he was obedient to his parents, beloved
of all, handsome, well-proportioned, gentle, modest, and

controlled, with none of the silly fads common to boys, but, as
St James the apostle says, 'swift to hear but slow to speak'.
He ministered with humble skill to all his father's visitors,
whether the king's companions or their slaves – a fine example of the prophet's dictum 'All shall be taught by the
Lord'. When he was fourteen he decided to leave his father's
estates to seek the Kingdom of Heaven, for his stepmother
was harsh and cruel. His own mother was dead. None the
less he managed to clothe, arm, and mount both himself and
his servants so that he need not feel ashamed in the royal
presence. His father blessed him, as Isaac blessed Jacob and
Jacob his own sons, that their seed might multiply a thousand
fold, and off he set to Eanfled, King Oswiu's queen, to be
presented to her on the recommendation of those noblemen
whom he had cared for at his father's house. Thanks be to
God, he at once found favour in her sight. He was handsome
and very keen-witted, so his request – to be allowed, on the
queen's advice and with her protection, to give himself to the
service of God – was granted. One of the king's most loving
and faithful companions, a nobleman called Cudda, had also
resolved, on account of his paralysis, to give up worldly am-
bition and dedicate himself to the monastic life at Lindisfarne. The queen commended the newly arrived Wilfrid
to him to join him in the service of God and act as his servant. Wilfrid set about his task with heartfelt zeal. This
and the fact that he strove humbly and obediently to carry
out the rule with sincere devotion made his master and
the older monks love him as a son, and his equals to regard
him as a brother. He learnt the whole psalter and several
other books by heart. His head was not yet tonsured but he
served God in purity and true circumcision of heart, deserving a share in the blessing which Samuel received as Eli's
servant.

## CHAPTER 3

*He longs to visit the threshold of St Peter,
Prince of the Apostles*

AFTER a year or two the youthful Wilfrid, prompted by the
Holy Ghost, conceived a great desire to visit the See of St

Peter, Prince of the Apostles, believing that he would wash
away every trace of sin thereby and receive a great blessing.
He told his master, who in his wisdom realized at once that
this longing came from God and gladly agreed that his dear
son should set out for the fount of all goodness. On Cudda's
advice, Queen Eanfled sent Wilfrid to her cousin Erconberht,
king of Kent. She fitted him out handsomely for the journey
and sent messages to convey her highest commendations of
him to Erconberht. There he was to stay until trustworthy
fellow-travellers might be found for him. When the king saw
this servant of God occupied, as was his wont, in constant
prayer and fasting, vigils and spiritual reading, he began
to love him dearly. Wilfrid had previously used St Jerome's
version of the psalms; now he learnt by heart the fifth edition,
the one in use in Rome. A whole year passed in tedious waiting, till at last, at the queen's prompting, the king found him
a guide in Bishop Baducing, a nobleman of outstanding intelligence, who was himself hastening Romewards. Like Jacob
he journeyed forth with his parents' blessing, a blessing
which was later to stand him in good stead. He was pleasant
to all, of keen mind, strong in body, willing to do any good
work, with never a sad look to cloud his face. He arrived
at Lyons in high spirits and broke the journey there with his
companions. Here his austere guide separated from him, just
as Barnabas took leave of Paul on account of John whose
surname was Mark.

## CHAPTER 4

*Archbishop Dalfinus makes him most welcome*

BLESSED be God, who protects and defends his servants and
sends good men to help them. In this city lived Archbishop
Dalfinus of happy memory. As soon as he set eyes on the
gentle Wilfrid and saw that his peaceful looks indicated a
saintly mind, he took a liking to him, and put up both him
and his companions as guests with all hospitality. He treated
them as though they were his own, provided them abundantly with all they needed, and expressed the wish to adopt
Wilfrid as his own son.

'Stay with me and be trustful,' he said, 'and I shall give you a good part of Gaul to govern in perpetuity and my own niece to be your wife. I shall adopt you as my son and you shall have me for a father and faithful helper in all things.'

The servant of God replied as wisdom had taught him.

'I have made my vows to the Lord and I shall keep them, leaving, like Abraham, my kinsfolk and my father's house to visit the Apostolic See, there to learn the laws of ecclesiastical discipline so that our nation may grow in the service of God. I yearn to receive the reward God promised to those that love Him when He said: "Everyone that hath forsaken father or mother shall receive a hundred fold and shall inherit ever-lasting life." If with God's help I am still alive, I promise to come back to see you.'

From this and other signs the holy bishop realized that he was a true servant of God and filled with the Holy Spirit. He provided him with his requirements for the journey and sent him off, as he wished, to the Apostolic See with guides and supplies.

### CHAPTER 5

*How he reaches the See of St Peter in safety*

WILFRID and his companions arrived after a good journey at their long-desired destination – the See of Peter, apostle and Prince of Apostles. Just as that most excellent Doctor of the Gentiles, St Paul, made his way to Jerusalem 'lest by any means I should run or had run in vain', so this most humble light of our race, stirred up by God 'to hear from the ends of the earth the wisdom' of this world's rulers, came to Rome. In the oratory dedicated to St Andrew he humbly knelt be-fore the altar over which the four gospels are placed, and adjured the apostle, by the name of the God for whom he had suffered, to obtain for him keenness of mind to learn and teach the nations the message of the Gospel. His prayer was granted, as many will testify. He passed many months in daily visits to the shrines of the saints, at one of which he found a teacher, sent by God and the apostle to be his faith-ful friend, Boniface the archdeacon, one of the wisest of

counsellors. Boniface made him word-perfect in the four
gospels, taught him the rule about Easter, of which the British
and Irish schismatics were ignorant, and many other rules of
Church law, teaching him as diligently as though he were his
own son. Later he presented him to the pope, giving a very
clear account of the whole purpose of this youthful servant of
God's journey. The pope placed his blessed hand on Wilfrid's
head, prayed over him, and blessed him. Then he set off in
the peace of Christ, armed with the holy relics he had collec-
ted in Rome, and so returned safely to his father the Archbishop of Lyons.

CHAPTER 6

*He receives the Roman form of tonsure from Archbishop*
*Dalfinus. The archbishop's martyrdom*

FINDING Archbishop Dalfinus safe and sound he went in
to greet him like a son, and recounted all the events of the
journey, one after another, to let him see how many blessings
he had received. The bishop thanked the Lord for having
watched over him in his travels and brought him safe home.
The boy stayed on for three years with him, making sound
progress under his learned tutors, and their love for each
other steadily grew. Wilfrid had an ardent desire to receive St
Peter's, that is the Roman, form of tonsure, which goes round
the head in the shape of Christ's own crown of thorns. The
archbishop gave it him. As he placed his hands on Wilfrid's
head he intended to make him his heir, should God will it;
but God had it in mind rather to benefit our own nation.

At that time the wicked Queen Baldhild was persecuting
the Church just like Jezebel who killed the prophets of old.
She spared priests and deacons but had nine bishops put to
death, one of whom was Dalfinus. The dukes, carrying out
their evil plan, ordered him to appear before them. He arrived quite undaunted at his trial, though he knew full well
what was coming. Our servant of God insisted on accompany-
ing him, despite Dalfinus's prohibition. With joy he exclaimed: 'What better than that father and son die at
once and go to Christ together!' The holy bishop received

the crown of martyrdom, but the dukes, seeing Wilfrid stripped and ready to receive his palm of martyrdom, asked who was the handsome youth preparing himself for death. 'A foreigner from across the sea, an Englishman,' they were told. 'Then do not lay hands on him. Spare him,' came their answer. So Wilfrid in his youth was already worthy to be counted a confessor* like St John the Evangelist, who sat unscathed in a cauldron of boiling oil and drank deadly poison without taking hurt.

<br>

CHAPTER 7

*The welcome he receives from Alhfrith*

ONCE his father Dalfinus had been buried with due honour, Wilfrid set sail with the relics of the saints and with many blessings to protect him. To the delight of the crew, a fair wind sprang up, giving them a pleasant voyage back to the haven of their native land. Alhfrith, who was reigning along-side his father Oswiu, got wind of Wilfrid's arrival, and hearing that he was an adherent of the true Easter rule and an expert in the discipline of the Church of St Peter (to which the king himself was greatly devoted), on the advice of his faithful friend Coenwalh, king of the West Saxons, he ordered him to appear before him. Wilfrid came and greeted him peacefully in the following words : 'Jesus Christ, the Son of God, commanded the disciples and their leader, the apostle Peter, saying : "Into whatsoever house ye enter, first say : Peace be to this house." We must first lay the foundations of this peace within ourselves and establish a harmony between body and soul, in obedience to St Paul's command : "Let the peace of Christ rule in your hearts." Then again Christ orders us to keep peace with our neighbour, saying : "Be wise and keep peace with one another." '

At the end of this address Alhfrith humbly prostrated himself at the feet of God's chosen servant, received his message, and asked for his blessing. He thought it was an angel of

* A saint who, though not a martyr, bore witness for Christ by a life of outstanding holiness.

God who spoke. Wilfrid blessed him and they talked together. The wisdom the king showed in his clever questions about details of discipline and government in the Roman Church was balanced every time by the learning and clarity of Wilfrid's answers. The king then begged him by the Lord and by St Peter to remain at court preaching the word of God to himself and the nation, as an organ, so to say, on which the Holy Spirit might play. Wilfrid realized the king's affection for him and agreed to stay. Then their souls intertwined in the most wonderful way, just as we read of David's soul being knit to Jonathan's.

## CHAPTER 8

### *Alhfrith gives him the monastery at Ripon*

THEIR love for each other increased daily. As a proof of this Alhfrith gave the saintly confessor Wilfrid about one thousand acres* of land at Stanforda† and then shortly afterwards, for his own soul's good, he gave him the monastery at Ripon and three thousand acres of land to go with it. Wilfrid was appointed abbot. This great opportunity for worldly aggrandizement – given by the Lord through the prayers of St Peter – Wilfrid used as a means of almsgiving: widow and orphan, the poor and those beset with any kind of infirmity, all benefited from his charity. You can tell from this that only lack of means had previously restricted his generosity. Behold with awe, my dear brethren, the benefit God bestowed on the king who 'found a goodly pearl and straightway bought it'. And the king was not alone in his love for Abbot Wilfrid; everyone, nobles and commons alike, looked on him as a prophet of God – which indeed he was.

* 'Ten hides'. The exact size of the hide in the seventh century is not known.
† See note, page 26.

## CHAPTER 9

### *Bishop Agilberht ordains him priest*

IN those days Agilberht, a bishop of foreign birth, visited Oswiu and Alhfrith. The latter pointed out Wilfrid to him, as someone who had come to him from the Apostolic See, and retailed the good reports he had heard from those who knew him – namely that he was humble, peaceable, given to prayer and fasting, kind, temperate, discreet, compassionate, full of the power and grace of God, modest, prudent, no wine-bibber, pure and open of speech, willing to learn and a good teacher.

'Therefore I beg you to raise him to the ranks of the priesthood and he and I shall be inseparable friends.'

To which Agilberht gave this prophetic reply: 'Such a man ought to be a bishop.'

He complied with the king's request by ordaining Wilfrid a priest at Ripon. Just as David was chosen by God as a boy, anointed by Samuel, and after many trials proved worthy to receive the gift of prophecy, so the holy priest Wilfrid, after many blessings from the saints of God, received gifts without number from God Himself, the guardian of his days of poverty.

## CHAPTER 10

### *The conflict between St Wilfrid the priest and Bishop Colman over the Easter Question*

ON a certain occasion while Colman was Bishop of York and metropolitan archbishop, during the reign of Oswiu and Alhfrith, abbots, priests, and clerics of every rank gathered at Whitby Abbey in the presence of the most holy Abbess Hilda, the two kings and Bishops Colman and Agilberht, to discuss the proper time for celebrating Easter: whether the practice of the British, Scots, and the northern province of keeping it on the Sunday between the fourteenth and twenty-second day of the moon was correct or whether they ought to give way to the Roman plan for fixing it for the Sunday between the fifteenth and twenty-first days of the moon. Bishop Colman, as was proper, was given the first chance to state his case. He spoke with complete confidence, as follows: 'Our fathers and theirs before them, clearly inspired by the Holy Spirit, as was Columba, stipulated that Easter Sunday should be celebrated on the fourteenth day of the moon if that day were a Sunday, following the example of St John the Evangelist "who leaned on the Lord's breast at supper", the disciple whom Jesus loved. He celebrated Easter on the fourteenth day of the moon, as did his disciples, and Polycarp and his disciples, and as we do on their authority. Out of respect to our fathers we dare not change, nor do we have the least desire to do so. I have spoken for our party. Now let us hear your side of the question.'

Agilberht, the foreign prelate, and his priest Agatho bade St Wilfrid, priest and abbot, use his winning eloquence to express in his own words the case of the Roman Church and Apostolic See. His speech was, as usual, humble.

'This question has already been admirably treated by a gathering of our most holy and learned fathers, three hundred and eighteen strong, at Nicaea, a city in Bithynia. Among other things they decided upon a lunar cycle recurring every nineteen years. This cycle gives no room for celebrating Easter on the fourteenth day of the moon. This is the rule followed by the Apostolic See and by nearly the whole world. At the end of the decrees of the fathers of Nicaea come these words: "Let him who condemns any one of these decrees be anathema." '

At the end of Wilfrid's speech Oswiu asked them, with a smile on his face, 'Tell me, which is greater in the Kingdom of Heaven, Columba or the apostle Peter ?'

Then the whole synod with one voice and one accord cried: 'The Lord Himself settled this question when He declared: "Thou art Peter and upon this rock I will build my Church and the gates of hell shall not prevail against it. And I will give you the keys of the Kingdom of Heaven; and whatsoever thou shalt bind on earth shall be bound in Heaven and whatsoever thou shalt loose on earth shall be loosed in Heaven." '

To this the king added, showing his wisdom: 'He is the keeper of the door and the keys. I will neither enter into strife and controversy with him, nor will I condone any who do. As long as I live I shall abide by his every decision.'

Bishop Colman was told that if, out of respect for his own country's customs, he should reject the Roman tonsure and method of calculating Easter, he was to resign his see in favour of another and better candidate. This he did.

## CHAPTER II

### *Wilfrid is elected to the episcopacy*

THE kings next consulted the councillors of the realm to decide upon whom to elect to the vacant see. The candidate must be of sterling character, acceptable to God and man, and willing both to make the discipline of the Apostolic See his own and to seek to spread it. Their choice was unanimous.

'No better nor worthier man could be found among us than Wilfrid, priest and abbot. He has proved himself wise in all things. We know him to be such as the apostle Paul describes to Titus: "For a bishop must be without crime, as the steward of God: not proud, not subject to anger, not given to wine, no striker, not greedy of filthy lucre; but given to hospitality, gentle, sober, just, holy, continent, embracing that faithful word which is according to doctrine, that he may be able to exhort in sound doctrine and to convince the gainsayers." He has every quality Paul thinks necessary. We therefore elect him in his prime of manhood to teach the law of God.' Like John the forerunner of the Lord and the prophet Ezekiel, he was chosen at the age of thirty. The election had the backing of the kings and of all the people; St Wilfrid was bidden to accept the rank of bishop in the Lord's name by the whole assembly. First of all he declined, on the grounds that he was not worthy. Later he thought it better to obey and not try to flee from God's blessing.

We who are still living hold exactly the same opinion about him as was current then.

In speech he was always pure and open, tempering

scrupulous regard for truth and solemnity of manner with a persuasive charm. His main topics of conversation were the mysteries of the law, the teachings of the faith, the virtue of continence, and the practice of right living. To everyone he gave different advice, advice always suitable to the individual character, for he knew, before ever he opened his mouth, exactly what to say and when and how and to whom to say it. He laid special emphasis on prayer, fasting, and vigils, and was forever searching the scriptures and studying the canons of the Church. He had a wonderful memory for texts. In imitation of the saints he spread peace among his brethren. He was full of humility and charity – charity which is worth far more than any other gift, without which every other virtue is vain. He cared for the poor, fed the hungry, clothed the naked, welcomed strangers, brought back captives, and protected the widow and orphan, all so that he might win the reward of eternal life amid the choirs of angels with Jesus Christ our Lord.

### CHAPTER 12

#### *How he comes to be consecrated in Gaul*

ON his election Wilfrid made the following speech.

'Your royal majesties, it behoves us to take careful thought as to how, with God's help but without criticism from Catholics, we, your candidate, might be raised to the episcopal dignity. Many English bishops are as much Quartodecimans* as the Celts themselves. Of course it is not for me to point the finger at them, but I know I am right. The Holy See does not consider the men they ordain as being in communion with her – any more than she does those who consort with schismatics. In all humility, therefore, let me beg you to send me, under your protection, across the sea to Gaul, where there are many bishops of recognized orthodoxy. There, though

---

* Quartodecimans were those who celebrated Easter on the fourteenth day of Nisan, irrespective of whether or not that day was a Sunday. Wilfrid must have realized the injustice of applying the name to the Celtic party; probably Eddius put it into Wilfrid's mouth as a smear.

unworthy, I can be consecrated without the Holy See raising
any objection.'

The kings approved and fitted him out with ship, supplies,
and a vast sum of money so that he might reach Gaul in
great state. Once he had arrived, a convention was formed
of at least fourteen Catholic bishops, Agilberht among them.
Having received his profession of faith, they consecrated him
before all the people with great satisfaction and no less pomp.
As their traditions demanded, he was borne into the oratory
aloft on a golden throne by nine bishops, to the accompani-
ment of songs and canticles from the choir. Shortly afterwards they sent him to the see of York, commanding him in
the Lord's name to keep the faith ; just as Paul had commanded his son Timothy to husband well the grace of God which
he had received through the laying on of his own hands.


CHAPTER 13

*The Lord delivers our bishop and his companions from
the sea and from the hands of pagans*


ON the crossing back from Gaul, Bishop Wilfrid's party in
mid-sea and in the middle of the clerics' songs and psalms of
praise, was alarmed by a sudden violent storm and contrary
winds, just like the disciples on the Lake of Galilee. The
wind howled from the south-east, and white-crested waves
hurled them towards the land of the South Saxons, a region
quite unknown to them. Then the waves left both men and
ship high and dry, and drained away from the land, laying
bare the shores, and receded far out to sea. Forthwith a great
horde of pagans approached, intending to seize the vessel,
loot it, carry off captives, and slay without more ado all who
resisted. Our holy bishop, anxious to save his friends' lives,
tried to pacify them with soothing words, and promised a
large sum of money. They were as fierce and stubborn as
Pharaoh ; they refused to let God's people free, declaring con-
temptuously that everything the sea cast on their shores was
theirs. The chief priest of their idolatry set himself up on a
high mound like Balaam and started to curse God's people,

trying to bind their hands by his magic art. One of the bishop's companions took a stone which all the people of God had blessed, and hurled it like David from a sling. It pierced the wizard's forehead through to the brain. Death took him as it took Goliath, unawares, and he fell back lifeless on the sand. The pagans then prepared for battle, but they directed their onslaught against God's people in vain, for God was on the side of the few. Gideon, at the Lord's command with three hundred warriors slew a hundred and twenty thousand of the Midianites in one attack. Our bishop's companions were small in number (only one hundred and twenty of them, one for each year of Moses' life) but, being stout-hearted and well armed, they formed a pact – that no one should turn his back and flee in battle but that each should either die with honour or live in triumph. God can grant either with equal ease. St Wilfrid and his clergy fell to their knees, raised their hands to heaven, and gained God's help. For just as Moses, Hur, and Aaron, lifting up his arms, called continually to the Lord for help while Joshua son of Nun did battle against Amalek, so did this little band of Christians vanquish a fierce and untamed pagan host. Thrice they routed them, with no mean slaughter, losing, strange to say, only five of their own men all told. Then St Wilfrid prayed again, and God sent back the tide sooner than usual; so that just as the pagans were preparing with all their might and main for a fourth battle, and their king had arrived, the sea flowed in over the whole beach, and the ship cast off and made for the deep. Thanking God for the glorious honour He had granted them, they had a fair passage with the south-west wind behind them and reached harbour at Sandwich.

### CHAPTER 14

*Chad, meanwhile, is ordained to Wilfrid's see*

As time went by without Wilfrid returning, King Oswiu, moved to envy by our ancient foe, ignorantly let the see be snatched by a candidate of the Quartodeciman party, a

highly irregular procedure and clean contrary to the mind
of the Apostolic See. This Chad, a Celt but a truly devout
servant of God and a great teacher, was ordained in complete defiance of canon law. Wilfrid knew nothing of the
whole affair. When he did return, it was easy to see who
was in the wrong, but Wilfrid withdrew to his old post
as abbot, to a humble life at Ripon for the next few years, remaining there all the time except for the frequent invitations
from King Wulfhere to carry out episcopal duties in Mercia.
Wulfhere had a sincere liking for him. God had raised up
for Himself this most gracious king – amongst whose good
works was the gift, for the good of his soul, of many pieces of
ground in various places to our bishop. Wilfrid soon used
them to found monasteries. Since Deusdedit, who followed
Archbishop Honorius, had died, the pious King Egbert of
Kent summoned Wilfrid to ordain a good number of priests
and deacons. One of these priests, Putta, later became a bishop
himself.

So Wilfrid carried on honourably, acting as bishop in
several areas and winning universal affection, and then returned to his own part of the country, bringing with him the
singers Aedde and Aeona and masons and artisans in every
kind of trade. He brought about a great improvement in the
church by introducing the Rule of St Benedict. He was another St Paul, opening in those parts the great door of the
faith.

### CHAPTER 15

*He regains his see*

AFTER three years had gone by, Archbishop Theodore came
from Kent to the king of Bernicia and Deira bringing with
him from Rome the decrees of the Apostolic See. As soon as
he set foot in the kingdom he was told how canon law had
been flouted, one bishop, like a thief, grabbing another's
diocese. He did not take this lightly. Chad was deposed.
Being an extremely meek man and a true servant of God, he
realized he had acted wrongly in being consecrated by those

Quartodecimans to someone else's see, humbly confessed his
fault, accepted the judgement of the bishops, and did penance. It was with Chad's consent then that Theodore installed
Wilfrid in York. Our holy bishop returned not wrong for
wrong but good for evil, following the Lord's command and
David's dealing with Saul where he says: 'I shall not lay
my hand upon the Lord's anointed.' His devoted friend
Wulfhere had given him Lichfield in Mercia, a place highly
suitable for an episcopal see either for himself or anyone he
might choose to give it to. So he made overtures of peace to
Chad, who was ready to pay the bishops complete obedience.
They ordained him through all the ecclesiastical degrees till
he was fully consecrated bishop and installed him at Lichfield, where he was given an honourable welcome by the
king. He lived a holy life rich in good works and, in due
course, went to his fathers, to await the coming of the Lord
in that judgement which, for him, ought to be extremely
lenient.

### CHAPTER 16

*The restoration of the church at York*

WHEN Wilfrid was installed at York during Wulfhere's
reign, the stonework of the church which had been first
founded and dedicated to God by St Paulinus, in the days of
that most Christian king, Edwin, was quite clearly half in
ruins. The top of the roof was too old to be serviceable any
longer; water streamed through it; the windows had never
been glassed in, so birds flew in and out and built their nests
inside; the walls were in a disgusting state, decaying and
filthy with the mess made by the birds and the rain. Our
holy bishop's soul stood still within him, like Daniel's, at the
sight of God's house, a house of prayer, looking like a den
of thieves. He planned to restore it and make it once more
pleasing to God. The decayed ridges of the roof were re-
placed; the craftsmen made a good job of them, covering
them with pure lead. The windows were glazed so that the
birds were excluded without shutting out the light too. The
walls were washed till they were in the words of the prophet,

'whiter than snow'. The interior of the building was decorated and the altar provided with all kinds of vessels. In addition to all this Wilfrid acquired vast tracts of land for the Church, thus relieving its poverty and enriching it with valuable endowments. What God said about Samuel and all the saints certainly applied to him: 'Whosoever will glorify me, him will I glorify', for he was loved and respected by the whole nation.

### CHAPTER 17

*The building and dedication of the church at Ripon*

IN the midst of all this worldly pomp there grew up in our bishop, by God's grace, an ever-increasing love for that Virgin Bride, the Church, espoused to one husband, the daughter of Charity which is the mother of all goodness. He decked her out with fair rules of discipline, as though with flowers of virtue, making her chaste and modest, continent and temperate and submissive, girt about with garments of every hue. In the words of the prophet, 'All the glory of the king's daughter is within.' Just as Moses, following the pattern God gave him on the mount, built with human hands a tabernacle of various hues to stir up the faith of Israel to the worship of God, so the most blessed Bishop Wilfrid, in the sight of all who believed in their heart and confessed their faith, adorned the bridal-chamber of the true Bridegroom and Bride with gold and silver and every shade of purple: at Ripon he started and completed from foundation to roof-beam a church built of dressed stone, supported with columns and complete with side aisles.

Like Solomon's temple it was consecrated on completion to the Lord and dedicated to St Peter, prince of the apostles, to gain the help of his prayers for all who might enter. The altar was dedicated and covered in purple woven with gold. The people participated in the ceremony and everything was carried out according to the canons. Those most devout and Christian kings, Ecgfrith and Aelwine, the kings beneath them, the abbots and sheriffs, and all kinds of dignitaries besides were present. Wilfrid stood in front of the altar, facing the people, and in the kings' presence read out in a clear voice a list of lands which previous monarchs and now themselves had given him for their souls' salvation with the consent and signature of the bishops and all the ealdormen. He went on to enumerate holy places in various parts of the country which the British clergy, fleeing from our own hostile sword, had deserted. God would indeed be pleased with the good kings for the gift of so much land to our bishop. They gave Wilfrid land round Ribble, Yeadon, Dent, and Catlow, and in other places too. When the sermon was over the kings started a feast of three days and nights in which all the people took part, showing kindness to their enemies and treating God's servants with deference. Our holy bishop adorned the house of God even further with a marvel of art hitherto undreamt of : he had had written, for his soul's good, a book of the gospels, done in letters of purest gold on parchment all empurpled and illuminated, and had ordered jewellers to make a case for them, also of the purest gold and set with precious gems. All these treasures and several more besides are kept in the church to this day as a memorial to him. His remains are here and his name is constantly remembered in the monks' daily prayer.

CHAPTER 18

*He restores a child to life*

'God is wonderful in his saints,' as the psalmist says; in their works His glory shines. We read in the Old Testament how God's servants did wonders in His name: Elias and Eliseus, for instance, raised the dead to life; and Christ's apostles, following their Master's example, drove out, as He promised they would, every kind of disease in His name. And now, to the glory of God, their successors, of whom our bishop is one, heal the afflicted in exactly the same way. St Wilfrid was out riding one day, going round on his various duties as bishop, baptizing and confirming. Among the people he baptized in the village of On Tiddanufri* was a

* Not identified.

certain woman. Her first born son had died and she was bitterly distressed, moaning with grief and tired out with the weight of the child – for she had the body with her, wrapped in rags and hidden in her bosom. She uncovered its face for the bishop to baptize it with the rest, hoping that it might be brought back to life. Our holy bishop saw that it was dead and stopped, at a loss what to do about it. The woman realized she was found out, fell to the ground, and wept bitterly, boldly adjuring him in the Lord's name to deliver her son from the lion's mouth by bringing him to life again to be baptized. She implored him more and more insistently by all the holiness of the episcopacy, kneeling and clasping his feet, kissing and bedewing them with her tears.

'Most holy lord,' she cried, 'do not dampen the faith of a bereaved woman. Strengthen my belief. Raise him up and baptize him and he shall live for God and for you. By the power of Christ do not delay.'

Then our holy bishop, in no doubt about the power of Christ and seeing in her the faith of the Syro-Phoenician woman, prayed and laid his hand on the corpse. The breath of life returned and the boy breathed again. He handed the child back to his mother, baptized him, and commanded her in God's name to give her son back to him at the age of seven for the service of God. The handsomeness of the boy and her husband's evil advice led the woman to break her promise when the time came. They fled the district. The bishop's reeve, Hocca, searched him out and found him living with a gang of Britons. He removed him by force and brought him to the bishop. The boy lived in the service of God and died in the great plague. How great and wonderful is the mercy of God who, through the power of his servant brought back to life a child dead and unbaptized so that, baptized, he might inherit a life of unending happiness in Heaven.

## CHAPTER 19

*The king's victory over the fierce Picts*

THE pious King Ecgfrith and Queen Aethilthryth were both obedient to Bishop Wilfrid in everything, and their reign was marked by fruitful years of peace and joy at home and victory over their enemies. Queen Aethilthryth's body did not corrupt in death, an indication that it was unstained in life.

Joas, the youthful king of Judah, during the lifetime of the great high-priest, Joada, pleased God and vanquished his enemies; when the priest died, however, he displeased the Lord and his kingdom diminished. This was the case with Ecgfrith too. While he was on good terms with the bishop, as many will tell you, he enlarged his kingdom by many victories; but when they quarrelled and the queen separated from him to give herself to God, the king's triumphs ceased, and that within his own lifetime. In the early years of his reign while the kingdom was still weak, the vicious tribes of the Picts fiercely resented their being subject to the Saxons; indeed they began to stir up revolt. Swarms of them gathered from every cranny of the north, like ants in summer sweeping up an earthwork to prevent their home from ruin. When the news reached Ecgfrith he quickly mustered a troop of cavalry and putting his trust in God, like Judas Maccabeus, set off with Beornhaeth, his trusty sub-king, and the little band of God's people against a vast army hidden in the hills. Ecgfrith was quite gentle with his people and merciful to his enemies, but quick in battle, impatient of delay. Host upon host of the enemy fell before him. He filled two rivers with the slain and his men crossed dry-shod over the corpses to slay the fugitives. Thus the Picts were reduced to slavery, a condition in which they remained until Ecgfrith himself was slain.

## CHAPTER 20

### *Ecgfrith's victory over the king of Mercia*

AFTER this Ecgfrith ruled his people with God's bishop in justice and holiness. He was David's equal for quelling his foes and God gave him yet more strength to temper the unruly spirit of the tribes who were rising under their warrior kings. Yet he walked humbly in the sight of the Lord, rendering Him thanks in all things. King Wulfhere of Mercia, a man of proud mind and insatiable will, stirred up all the southern nations against our own, intent not merely on war but meaning even to enslave us to him as tributaries. His designs were not inspired by God. So Ecgfrith, king of Bernicia and Deira, a man of unwavering purpose, took the advice of his counsellors, followed the injunctions of his bishop, put his trust in God and marched forth against the enemy host, in defence of Church and fatherland, with as few troops as had Barak and Deborah. With God's help he laid them low. Countless numbers were slaughtered, their king routed, and the Kingdom of Mercia itself put under tribute. Later Wulfhere died (I do not know the exact cause) and Ecgfrith ruled a wider realm in peace.

## CHAPTER 21

### *Our bishop's virtue*

THESE conquests at one and the same time extended our most pious King Ecgfrith's territory and enlarged the field of Wilfrid's ecclesiastical jurisdiction. He was now bishop of the Saxons in the south and of the British, Scots, and Picts to the north. He was dearly loved by every race, performed his duties as bishop with all diligence, ordained priests and deacons to help him in all parts of the diocese, and steered the barque of the Church on an even keel through the tossing billows of this world. No wave of conviviality swamped him;

neither did he let his abstinence cast him against the rocks of
pride. He was habitually temperate at feasts – and even when
alone never drank a full glass, no matter how small the vessel might be, neither summer nor winter, whether parched
with thirst or faint with cold. There are plenty of witnesses
to vouch for this. In praying and keeping vigil, in spiritual
reading and in fasting, where will you find his equal? He
himself testified before the faithful that he had kept his body
unspotted from his mother's womb. Every night, summer and
winter, he washed himself in holy water until Pope John of
happy memory advised him to forgo such rigours on account
of his age. Nearly all the abbots and abbesses made over their
possessions to him by vow, either retaining them in his name
during their lifetime or naming him heir in their wills.
Nobles, men of high position in the world, sent their sons for
him to tutor so that they might have the choice either of giving themselves to God or else of returning as grown men
with Wilfrid's recommendation to enter the king's service as
warriors. These things only served to kindle the flame of
envious hate in many hearts, a flame which the devil was
quick to fan; but our holy bishop, carrying, in the words of
St Paul, armour on the right arm and on the left, bore with
equanimity both good fortune and bad. His gifts both to
clergy and laity were on such a grand scale that he was second
to none in largesse.

## CHAPTER 22

### The building of the house of God at Hexham (672–8)

HE cleaved to God unceasingly, as the psalmist says, placing
his hope in the Lord, sweetly rendering his vows to Him to
whom he owed everything. At Hexham he built a church to
the glory of God and the honour of St Andrew on land
given by the saintly Queen Aethilthryth. My poor mind is
quite at a loss for words to describe it – the great depth of
the foundations, the crypts of beautifully dressed stone, the
vast structure supported by columns of various styles and

with numerous side-aisles, the walls of remarkable height and length, the many winding passages and spiral staircases leading up and down. Without a doubt it was the Spirit of God who taught our bishop to plan the construction of such a place, for we have never heard of its like this side of the Alps. Bishop Acca, who by God's grace is still with us, decked out this superb edifice with splendid gold and silver ornaments, precious stones and silks and purples for the altars. What description could do justice to the fabric he installed?

## CHAPTER 23

### *He heals a half-dead boy*

DURING the construction of the highest parts of the walls of the church, a young man, one of the bishop's masons, lost his footing on a high pinnacle, fell headlong, and dashed himself on the stone pavement below. He broke his arms and legs; every joint was put out. There he lay gasping his last. The masons thought he was dead and at the bishop's command, took him outside on a bier. Wilfrid had been praying and weeping but now hastily summoned all the workmen.

'Let us show how great our faith is by praying together with one accord that God may send back the soul into this lad's body and hear our prayers for his life, even as he heard the prayers of St Paul.'

They knelt down and prayed that he who mocks at every good thing might have no victory to gloat over in this building. The bishop prayed after the manner of Elias and Eliseus and gave his blessing. The breath of life returned to the boy. The doctors bound up his arms and legs and he improved steadily day by day. He is still alive to give thanks to God and his name is Bothelm.

## CHAPTER 24

*How envy is stirred up against our bishop and he is
driven from his see*

THE tempter, 'like a roaring lion', to quote St Peter, went
prowling round God's fold looking for an entry, on the watch
both night and day, trying to overcome the strongest soldier
first – for, that done, the rest would easily be conquered. In
this skirmish he chose his usual weapon, one by which he has
often spread defilement throughout the whole world – woman. Iurminburgh, Ecgfrith's queen, greatly envied Bishop
Wilfrid. Later, let me tell you, after the king was killed,
she changed from a she-wolf into a lamb of God indeed, a
perfect abbess and mother of her community. But now she
corrupted the king's heart with poisonous tales about Wilfrid,
imitating Jezebel in her onslaughts on the prophets and in
her persecution of Elias. She used all her eloquence to describe to Ecgfrith all St Wilfrid's temporal glories, listing his
possessions, the number of his monasteries, the vastness of
the buildings, his countless followers arrayed and armed like
a king's retinue. Her darts pierced the king's heart and took
effect; from then on the pair of them used their cunning to
secure the condemnation of this holy head of the church
and to snatch all the gifts left to God by former kings. This
certainly showed daring on their part, but in the end their
ill-will turned back upon themselves. Balak went against
God's will when he summoned Balaam to help him. They
did likewise. They secured Archbishop Theodore to further
criminal folly, winning him over with bribes, for money will
blind even the wisest. Theodore came to them and heard them
explain that they intended to humiliate Wilfrid. Without the
least excuse he agreed to condemn him although he was completely blameless. While our bishop was absent, Theodore
found three men from somewhere or other, not Wilfrid's
subjects, and in flagrant contempt of law and precedent
proceded to conscecrate them bishops over Wilfrid's own
territory. Our holy bishop, when the news reached him, went

straight to the king and the archbishop to find out why, when there was no charge against him, his enemies should behave like robbers and defraud him of all the wealth which the kings, for their love of God, had left him. This is the famous public reply he received: 'We do not find you guilty of any crime whatsoever; none the less our decrees against you are to remain unchanged.'

This disgraceful decision by no means satisfied our bishop, and on the advice of his fellow bishops he decided to take the case to the Holy See; just as Paul appealed to Caesar when condemned without reason by the Jews. As he turned away from the royal tribunal, he said to the king's minions who were smirking with delight at his defeat: 'You who are now laughing at my malicious condemnation will be shedding bitter tears a year from today.'

And his prophecy was true. For twelve months later, to the day, the corpse of King Aelfwini was carried into York, at the sight of which the whole population wept and tore their hair for grief and rent their garments.

CHAPTER 25

*Bishop Winfrid of Lichfield is robbed*

WILFRID prepared to set sail with his companions and some of his clergy. The many thousands of monks he was forced to leave behind in the power of the upstart bishops mourned and bewept their fate, imploring God to direct their bishop's journey according to His will. Wilfrid's enemies, finding more scope for their malice in the supposition that he was bound for Etaples and thence by the direct route to Rome, sent envoys off with bribes to Theodoric, King of the Franks, and the wicked Duke Ebroin. They were either to exile him for good or kill his friends and take all his possessions. The Lord freed him from his enemies as though from the hands of Herod himself, for just then Bishop Winfrid, who had been driven out of Lichfield, happened to be on the selfsame route. He fell into their hands and may as well have fallen into the lion's jaws, for they seized him, took all his money, killed many of his friends, and inflicted the extremes of misery on him by leaving him naked. Luckily for our bishop they had mistaken the first syllable of Winfrid's name.

## CHAPTER 26

### *His journey takes him to Friesland*

FAR from being molested, our holy bishop and his companions were gently wafted on by a westerly breeze and, with prows dipping towards the east, arrived after a pleasant journey at the coast of Friesland, to be received with all ceremony by King Aldgisl and vast crowds of the heathen. With the king's permission Wilfrid preached daily to the people in the open air, telling them openly about the true God, the Father Almighty, and Jesus Christ His Only Begotten Son and the Holy Spirit who is co-eternal with Him. He preached one baptism for the remission of sin and the resurrection after death to life everlasting. In the pagans' eyes his doctrine gained strong backing by the fact that his arrival was marked by an unusually large catch of fish. Indeed the year was an abnormally fruitful one for every kind of produce. All this they attributed to the glory of the God whom the holy man was preaching. So his preaching was accepted and that year he baptized all but a few of the chiefs and many thousands of the common people, thus laying like the Apostle of the Gentiles the foundation of the faith upon which his son is still building. By his son I mean Willibrord, who was nurtured at Ripon and is now, by God's grace, a bishop. At present he is wearing himself out with toil, but shall have his reward above.

## CHAPTER 27

### *The king refuses the price set upon Wilfrid*

AT that time Ebroin, one of the dukes of Theodoric, King of the Franks, sent messengers with letters for Aldgisl, greeting him with words of peace and promising on oath a full bushel of gold solidi – a foul offer indeed – if he would send Wilfrid

to him alive, or slay him and send his head. The king had
the letter read out for all to hear, including ourselves and the
messengers, who were feasting with his people in the palace
at the time. When it had been read out he took the scroll and
tore it up for all to see and threw the pieces on to a fire blazing
in front of him. He gave the bearers this message: 'Tell your
lord what you now hear me say: Thus may the Creator of all
things rend and destroy the life and lands of him who per-
jures himself before God and breaks the pact he has made.
Even thus may he be torn to pieces and burn to ashes.'

The messengers left in confusion at the king's refusal to
countenance the crime, and returned to their master.

CHAPTER 28

*Wilfrid is welcomed by kings Dagobert and Perctarit*

OUR beloved bishop (and God's) spent the winter with the
Frisians and gained many souls for Christ. At the first sign
of spring he and his companions continued on their journey
to the Holy See. They came to Dagobert, king of the Franks,
and were most graciously received. This courtesy was a return
for former favours from Wilfrid. Dagobert had been banished in his youth by enemies who were then on the throne.
He sailed away, his fortune ruined, and came, by God's help,
to Ireland. Years later his friends and relatives learnt from
travellers that he was alive, flourishing and in the prime of
manhood, and sent to Wilfrid to ask him to invite Dagobert
across from Scotland or Ireland and then to send him over
to them as their king. This our holy bishop did; he made
him welcome on his arrival from Ireland, provided him with
arms and sent him back in great state with a troop of his companions to support him. The king did not forget such kindness. He now begged Wilfrid to accept the chief bishopric of
the realm, Strasbourg; and when Wilfrid declined, he sent
him on his way with lavish presents and with his own bishop,
Deodatus, to guide him. They journeyed on under God's
guidance till they came to Perctarit, king of Campania, a
gentle humble man, and one who held God's word in awe.

159

He received them graciously, as God bade, and gave Wilfrid this news: 'Your enemies sent messengers to me from Britain with greetings and the promise of a great reward if I would lay hands upon you as a bishop in secret flight (for so they describe you) and keep you from reaching the Apostolic See. I refused to take part in such a scandalous plot. This was the answer I gave them: "As a youth I was exiled from my own country and found refuge with a king of the Huns, a pagan. Before the idol he called his God he made a pact with me never to hand me over or betray me to my enemies. Some time afterwards messengers came from my enemies promising on oath a full bushel of gold solidi if he would hand me over to be slain. He refused, declaring that his gods would cut short his life if he broke his promise to them by this foul deed. How much more then must I, who know the true God, refuse to send my soul to perdition rather than gain even the whole world?"'

In thanksgiving for his own safekeeping Perctarit treated Wilfrid with great honour and sent him off with guides towards his long desired goal, Rome.

CHAPTER 29

*Our bishop's letters are received by the most blessed Pope Agatho and the holy synod*

God's beloved bishop reached Rome quite safely, only to learn that his case had preceded him; the holy monk Cenowald had just then arrived with letters from Archbishop Theodore. So Pope Agatho was already familiar with the quarrel. To an assembled gathering of holy bishops and priests, more than fifty in number, in that church of our Lord and Saviour Jesus Christ which is called the Basilica of Constantine, the most holy and thrice blessed Agatho, bishop of the Holy Catholic and Apostolic Roman Church, gave the following address: 'The reason why I have summoned you, venerable brethren, is not hidden from you. I require this honourable assembly to understand and discuss with me the dissension which has recently arisen among the churches in the island of Britain, where through God's grace the company of the faithful has greatly increased. News of the quarrel has come both from pilgrims' accounts of the situation and from a series of written reports.'

Andrew, the most reverend Bishop of Ostia and John, Bishop of Porto, then rose to speak.

'The ordering of the affairs of all the churches hangs on the decision of your apostolic authority. You fulfil the office of the blessed apostle Peter to whom the Creator and Redeemer of all, Christ Our Lord, gave the keys for loosing and binding. In accordance with your Holiness's recent injunction, sitting in session with our brother bishops and fellow servants we have read every letter which the messengers from Britain brought to your Holiness, as well as those which have come from Archbishop Theodore, who was himself formerly sent to Britain by the Apostolic See, and the reports from others against a certain bishop who, they allege, secretly fled from his diocese and whom they believe to have come to Rome. We have gone through those presented by Wilfrid, Bishop of York and God's beloved, who has come here to appeal to the Apostolic See against ejection from his diocese by the above-mentioned holy archbishop. In these letters the accusers raise many dubious points, but never do we find Wilfrid convicted of any crime at all, on any interpretation of the sacred canons, and therefore the ejection was completely irregular. His accusers' statements cannot prove him guilty of anything leading to his degradation. Rather are we of the opinion that he refrained by his modesty from implicating himself in seditious quarrelling. After being ejected, he let his fellow bishops know the merits of the case and forthwith had recourse to the Apostolic See wherein Christ the Almighty Lord who redeemed the Church with His Blood founded the primacy of the priesthood and confirmed the authority of the Prince of the Apostles. Finally the case has been submitted to your apostolic jurisdiction for an authoritative answer.'

Then Agatho, the most holy and thrice blessed bishop of the Holy Catholic Roman Church, thus replied: 'Wilfrid,

Bishop of York and God's beloved, is said to be at the doors of this assembly. Let him, in answer to his request, be admitted to address the petition he has brought.'

Our beloved bishop, on entering the sacred precincts, began: 'I beseech your Pontifical Holiness to command that this my humble petition be received and read out in your presence.'

To this the pope replied: 'Let Bishop Wilfrid's petition be received and read out before the whole gathering.'

It was then taken and read out in front of the whole apostolic council by John the notary.

## CHAPTER 30

### *The text of the petition*

'I WILFRID, a humble and unworthy English bishop, with God going before to guide me, have directed my steps to this the apostolic citadel, as though to a fortress and a tower of strength, because I am confident that in that place from which the rules of the sacred canons emanate and are diffused throughout all the churches of the world to be handed down through the preaching of the bishops and received with a lively faith – there, I repeat, am I sure to be given a just judgement, unimportant though I am. I do not doubt that your Holiness has taken note both of what I stated in my letters and what I have claimed here and now in your presence; and, furthermore, I alleged when I was presented to your Holiness on arrival, that certain invaders had had the presumption to go entirely against the declared ruling of the canons and, at a synod consisting of the most holy Archbishop Theodore of Canterbury and other bishops, had, like thieves, attempted to assail the see which I, by God's mercy, had ruled for ten years and more. They succeeded in robbing me, planting themselves in my place and being consecrated as bishops. There is not just the one usurper, there are three of them. Their consecrations were, naturally, uncanonical. Because of the respect due to the archbishop I pass over the question how so venerable a man could have brought himself to consecrate, without any bishop's consent, and in face of my respectful opposition, three bishops to the see of York while I was still alive. I would rather not labour the point, for I hardly dare accuse the envoy of the Apostolic See. Should it be made clear, however, that I have been cast out of my see in contempt of the law by my enemies' spite without ever being convicted of any crime, without being guilty on any count whatsoever, let alone those for which the law reserves its severities, and should it be further proved (as I can assure you it can) that, once thrown out, I neither stirred up quarrels and sedition nor set myself to oppose my enemies but at once sought help from the Holy See, having simply protested to my fellow bishops before departure – if all this is proved and yet your Holiness and the council of bishops decide that though blameless I am still to be considered deposed, then I shall embrace your decision with humble devotion. But if I am to be restored to my diocese, I shall follow and venerate that decision with all my strength, provided you issue a decree sanctioning the ejection of the usurpers. If, on the other hand, you should think fit to appoint other bishops to my diocese, then let them be such as I can serve God with in unity, peace, and concord, so that each of us may recognize the established laws of the Church and take care to guard the flock committed to him. If it pleases the archbishop and my fellow bishops to increase the number of bishops, then let men be chosen from our own clergy, candidates whom the bishops in synod can agree upon. Do not let the Church suffer damage from strangers and outsiders; anything irregular and imprudent does nothing but give rise to quarrel after quarrel, such as can never be unravelled, appeased, nor ended. I trust that I show absolute obedience to and full compliance with the laws of the Church – to whose justice I have hastened with full confidence, having put all other matters aside in order to do so.'

## CHAPTER 31

### *Pope Agatho's answer*

THE most holy and thrice blessed Agatho, Bishop of the Holy Catholic and Apostolic Church of the city of Rome, replied thus: 'It has been a great source of satisfaction to realize, as the petition was taking its course, that Bishop Wilfrid, God's beloved, did not let his belief that he had been unjustly ejected from his see drive him into contumacious opposition, to meet, as the world would, force with force. Rather did he humbly bethink himself to seek the canonical remedies from our holy founder, St Peter, the Prince of the Apostles. Moreover he meekly awaits the decision, promising prompt obedience without cavil, vowing wholehearted assent to whatever Peter, whose office we perform, shall declare through our lips.'

## CHAPTER 32

### *The synod's reply*

THE whole synod, headed by Pope Agatho and exercising its lawful authority, promulgated, among its various decrees, the following decision:

'We decree and lay down that Bishop Wilfrid, God's beloved, is to take possession of the see which until recent times was his, according to the terms previously defined. He will summon a council to help him choose coadjutors, men with whom he will be able to live without friction, as the existing rule demands. These are to be consecrated by the archbishop. Those who, in defiance of the law, have taken over in his absence are to be expelled without hesitation. If anyone should be rash enough to attempt to resist these statutes of the synod or refuse to obey them or at any later date should try to infringe them in whole or in part, then, without regard to either their present or future rank, they shall be overthrown. This we enjoin on the authority of the prince of the apostles.

If it be a bishop who dares to flout this holy ordinance, let him be degraded from episcopal rank and be forever anathema, and similarly with priest or deacon or minor cleric. Indeed, whether he be cleric, monk, or layman of any degree, even king, let him be made an outcast from the Body and Blood of our Saviour Jesus Christ; may he not be counted worthy to look upon Him at His awful Second Coming. But he who with sincere devotion and complete accord receives, holds, and carries out or helps to bring to perfection these our ordinances, may he see 'the goodness of the Lord in the land of the living', may his part be with those who sit at God's right hand, may he possess eternal beatitude and, with all those who have won favour in the sight of God and gained unending glory, may he be found worthy to hear, as a reward for that obedience which God prizes beyond all sacrifice, the divine voice of Our Lord Jesus Christ, the Universal Judge, pronounce the words: "Come ye blessed of my father, inherit the kingdom prepared for you from the foundation of the world." '

## CHAPTER 33

### *Our bishop returns*

WILFRID's long stay in Rome was brought to an end by the injunction of the pope and synod to return home, taking with him the orders of the Holy See which he was to show to Archbishop Theodore and King Ecgfrith. Our holy bishop carried out these commands with unwavering loyalty as he had promised, but before setting out he spent several days going round the shrines of the saints making his devotions. He managed to obtain, much to the comfort of the churches of Britain, a large supply of relics, each of which he labelled with a description of the object itself and the name of the saint. In his usual way he acquired numerous other articles to decorate the house of God, but it would be tedious to give a list of them all here. Finally he and his company set out for home in great joy with the blessing of pope and synod and with the help of God. He journeyed on, bearing the triumphal decision, up through Campania and over the mountains till he came to the land of the Franks, only to find that his faithful friend King Dagobert had been assassinated by some treacherous dukes and (Heaven defend us!) with the bishops' consent. One of these same prelates rode out to meet Wilfrid at the head of a mighty army, intending, had not God intervened, to rob the whole company, reduce them to serfdom or sell them into slavery, and to kill any who resisted. Our holy bishop was to suffer the anguish of being imprisoned and reserved for Duke Ebroin's judgement.

'What made you so bold,' they demanded, 'as to pass through the land of the Franks, seeing that you deserve to be put to death for making Dagobert king? You it was who brought him back from exile and what did he do but lay waste our cities, spurn the advice of our elders, act like Solomon's son Rehoboam in imposing an humiliating tribute on his people, and despise the Church of God and her rulers? These are the crimes for which he was slain; this is the reason his body now lies in the grave.'

Our holy bishop answered humbly: 'In the name of Jesus Christ what I say is true; by the holy apostle Peter I swear I do not lie. It was in accordance with God's command to the people of Israel when they dwelt as strangers in a foreign land that I helped and cherished King Dagobert, then an exile and a wanderer. I raised him up not to your harm but for your good, sending him to build up your cities, to put spirit into your citizens, to counsel your senate, and, as he promised in the Lord's name, to defend the Church. Most righteous bishop, if an exile of my own country, and one of royal blood, had come to your lordship, where else would your duty have lain?'

The prelate replied: 'The Lord preserve your goings out and your comings in. Woe to me, sinner that I am! Pardon me, for, like the patriarch Judah, I see you are more righteous than I. The Lord be with you, and may the apostle Peter be your aid.'

## CHAPTER 34

### *The king flouts the decisions of the Holy See*

AFTER having covered a great distance on land, and with the help of God and a ship traversed the wide ocean, he and all his train arrived at their native shore alive and unscathed, to the unbounded joy of his subjects who had been languishing and calling out with tears to the Lord for their absent bishop. He returned bearing the standard of victory, that is the decision of the Apostolic See, and peaceably presented himself before the king to show him the written judgement of the pope in which the whole synod had concurred and which each member had signed. He delivered the document all stamped with bulls and seals, then summoned the clergy and principal inhabitants of the district to the place where the synod usually met and there read out to them the decrees of of the Apostolic See, sent from Rome to bring back peace to the churches. Some of them, because the document contained proposals that went against the grain or which they simply refused to accept, contumaciously rejected it. Others – and this is far more detestable – imperilled their souls by alleging that those very letters which the Holy See had sent to comfort them had been obtained through bribery. Then, at the command of king and counsellors and with the consent of the bishops who had usurped his see, Wilfrid was condemned to prison for nine months, there to be kept without any mark of honour to his rank. No sooner had the letters been opened and read out than – the very thought makes us tremble – the king flew into a rage and, urged on by his flattering minions, defied the judgement of St Peter, of him to whom God gave the power of loosing and binding; not content with this he swore by his soul's health that Wilfrid should be despoiled of all but his clothes and put in solitary confinement, that his subjects be scattered far and wide and no friend be allowed to come near him. The queen, moreover, took away his reliquary full of relics of the saints and – I can hardly bear to tell it – wore it as a necklace both at home in her chamber and when she rode forth in her chariot. But this foul deed brought her nothing but harm, just as befell the Philistines when, after routing the people of Israel, they carried off the ark and dragged the Holy of Holies through their cities.

## CHAPTER 35

### *Wilfrid encourages his brethren*

WILFRID, God's beloved, addressed his comrades thus: 'Keep in mind and recall to the brethren those days of old, how we read in the Old Testament that God's beloved patriarchs and his firstborn, Israel, "passed from nation to nation and from one kingdom to another", awaiting the promise and not despairing. Moses too and Aaron and all the prophets of God endured men's persecution, for their trust was in the Lord. In the New Testament we read how the great Shepherd of the Sheep and Head of the Whole Church, Jesus Christ, was crucified by the Jews and his disciples scattered. Later, dispersed throughout the entire world, they and their followers after various tribulations received the crown of martyrdom. They did not forget those words of comfort which are addressed to us too as His sons, in the epistle to the Hebrews: "My son, neglect not the discipline of the Lord; neither be thou wearied whilst thou art rebuked by him. For whom the Lord loveth he chastiseth and he scourgeth every son whom he receiveth." So, brethren and helpers in Christ, in the words of that same epistle, "Let us also who have so great a cloud of witnesses over our head run with patience the race that is set before us." '

## CHAPTER 36

### *Of the house lit up by God*

WILFRID'S words of consolation ended, the king's officers led our holy bishop away like a lamb to the slaughter

to Osfrith, sheriff of the royal borough of Broninis.*
He was confronted with the prisoner and bidden, on the
king's command, to take our holy bishop into custody. Wilfrid, whose faith was so great by now that he might well have
been called the light of Britain, was to be locked up in a pitch-
black dungeon and securely guarded, and all this was to be
kept secret from his friends. The sheriff, in loyalty to the
king, carried out his urgent command. Wilfrid was hidden
away, under guard, in a place which was rarely brightened
by the sun during the day and where no lamp was lighted to
grace the hours of the night. His guardians, hearing him continually singing psalms, looked into the cell and found the
darkness of the night turned into day. Thunderstruck themselves they terrified others with the tale of his holiness.

'O Christ, Eternal light, who dost not desert those who
acknowledge Thee, Thou whom we believe to be the true
light illuminating "every man that cometh into this world",
who in the beginning didst mark with fiery glory the hour of
thy future servant's birth when he came forth from his mother's womb, now as he prayed in the darkness of his prison
cell Thou didst deign to send an angel to visit him and to
bring him light, just as when Thine apostle Peter was imprisoned in chains by wicked Herod. To Thee be glory and
thanksgiving!'

While he was languishing in prison without the least token
of respect, the king sent to offer him what was part of his
own diocese and other very lavish gifts provided he acquies-
ced in the king's commands and ordinances and denied that
the statutes sent by Rome were genuine. To this he humbly
replied, showing his trust in the authority of the Holy See,
that he would rather lose his head than assent to such a
proposal. From this we can learn that a strong will founded
on the knowledge of God cannot be confounded.

*Not identified.

## CHAPTER 37

### *He heals a woman*

WHILE our holy bishop was waiting patiently in prison he was honoured with miracles, just as St John the Evangelist during his confinement on Patmos was granted visions of the mighty works of God. For at this time when, as we have said, Wilfrid was in a sorry plight, the sheriff's wife was suddenly taken ill. She went quite stiff, lost all feeling in her limbs, went cold and began to foam at the mouth, then lost consciousness and was almost breathing her last. The sheriff, realizing she was dying, rushed to Wilfrid like the centurion ran to Our Lord; he knelt before him confessing his faults and admitting the king's wrongdoing, and begged Wilfrid in God's name to help him, unworthy as he was, by coming to his dying wife. Our bishop harboured no malice. He went to the poor woman, and, standing over her, sprinkled her face with holy water. Then, calling on the Lord for help, he poured the water drop by drop into her mouth until it was well moistened. The woman opened her mouth and took deep breaths. She opened her eyes and consciousness and understanding returned. After a while warmth came back to her limbs, and she was able to raise her head and move her tongue. She thanked God aloud and then, like Peter's mother-in-law, ministered to our holy pontiff. She is still living and is now an abbess having taken the name of Aebbe in religion. She often recounts this story with tears.

## CHAPTER 38

### *His chains fall off him*

THIS same sheriff did not dare treat his prisoner decently, for fear of the king, nor, out of respect for his holiness and for fear of God's wrath, did he dare ill treat him. So he sent a message to his master.

'I implore you,' it went, 'by my life and salvation, not to force me to imperil my soul by having to punish this holy and innocent bishop any further. I would rather die than scourge him, for he is guiltless.'

This maddened the king. In reply he sent Wilfrid to his town of Dunbar under the supervision of a sheriff called Tydlin whom he knew to be more cruel. Wilfrid, despite his personal holiness and exalted rank, was to be bound hand and foot and not permitted contact with anyone. Tydlin obeyed and ordered the smiths to forge iron fetters. These smiths, with deliberate malice, put their heart into the work, but God worked against them. The irons always turned out either too small and narrow or else so big and loose that they slipped off the wrists and ankles of God's baptist and evangelist. This terrified the guards so much that they left him unbound. He sang psalms and gave thanks to the Lord unceasingly, 'Enduring,' in St Paul's words to the Hebrews, 'a great buffeting by afflictions, by reproaches made a gazing-stock, undergoing with joy the robbery of all his goods'; and in Wilfrid's case the suffering had been inflicted by his own fellow-countrymen. Thus his jailers, much against their will, were forced to confine him unbound until God's appointed time.

CHAPTER 39

*How the queen falls ill and is healed*

In the meantime the king and queen were making their progress through the cities, fortresses, and villages with worldly pomp and daily feasts and rejoicings, in the course of which they came to the nunnery of Coldingham. The abbess, King Oswiu's sister Aebbe, was a very wise and holy woman. At this same place the queen was possessed by a devil during the night and, as in the case of Pilate's wife, the attacks were so severe that she was hardly expected to last till day. As dawn was breaking the abbess came to the queen and found her lying with the muscles of her limbs all contracted and screwed up. Obviously she was dying. Off went Abbess Aebbe to the

king and with tears in her eyes gave her opinion of the cause
of the calamity. Indeed she rounded on him.

'I know for a fact that you ejected Wilfrid from his see for
no reason at all. He was driven into exile and went to Rome
to seek redress. Now he has returned from that see that has
the same power as St Peter himself in loosing and binding.
And what have you done but stupidly despised its injunctions
and despoiled the bishop? Then to pile injury on injury you
have had him locked away in jail. Listen, my son, to your
mother's advice. Loosen his bonds. Restore the relics your
queen has taken from his neck and carried round from city
to city like the ark of the Lord to her own doom. Send a messenger with them now. The best plan would be to reinstate
him as bishop, but if you cannot bring yourself to do this,
then at least let him and his friends leave the kingdom and
go where they will. Do this and, as I see it, you will live and
your queen will recover. Disobey and, as God is my witness,
you shall not escape punishment.'

The king obeyed the holy matron, freed our bishop, and
let him depart with his relics and all his friends. And the
queen recovered.

## CHAPTER 40

### *Wilfrid is welcomed by Berhtwald*

So Wilfrid and his companions left their native land and set
off in exile for the kingdoms of the south. God, who does not
leave his saints to endure alone, sent a kind-hearted man to
meet them on their way, a sheriff of noble birth called Berhtwald, nephew to Aethilred King of Mercia. As soon as he
saw such honourable men and ascertained the reason for their
wanderings he begged them in God's name to come and stay
with him. He insisted that they accept part of his estate to
settle down on. Wilfrid sincerely thanked God for having
given him the consolation of somewhere to rest and without
delay founded a little monastery. His monks occupy it to
this day. But, alas, the ancient enemy was always on the
alert and King Aethilred and his queen, Ecgfrith's sister,

hearing that Wilfrid had been staying there awhile in peace, forbade Berhtwald, as he valued his safety, to harbour him another day. They did this to flatter Ecgfrith. The monks remained, but Wilfrid was spitefully driven out and made his way to Centwini, King of the West Saxons. He was not long there either for persecution followed him. Centwini's queen, Queen Iurminburgh's sister, detested him, so, because of the three kings we have mentioned, he was forced to move on yet again.

### CHAPTER 41

*The conversion of the pagans of Selsey*

But I am making the tale drag. His release from prison and exile from his own province brought him no peace, for Ecgfrith stirred up unremitting persecution against him in every country on both sides of the Channel, as far as his power and influence extended. There was but one place free, an area of Sussex which dense forests and rocky coast had saved from conquest by other kingdoms. Up to this time it had remained persistently heathen, and thither God, when all human aid failed, directed our good bishop's steps. He sought out King Aethilwalh and told him the whole story of his hardships and exile. Aethilwalh made a pact with him at once, swearing such friendship as neither threat nor sword of any of Wilfrid's enemies nor any amount of bribes should ever frighten or tempt him into breaking. The holy man of God, delighted with these words of consolation, gave thanks to God and began gently to persuade the king and queen to accept the word of God, preaching to them the greatness and blessedness of God's Kingdom, giving them, as it were milk without guile. Next, with divine permission and royal consent and at Wilfrid's exhortation, the people, who never before had had the gospel preached to them, were gathered together. Our holy bishop standing in the midst of the pagans exclaimed in the manner of our Lord Jesus Christ and his forerunner St John the Baptist: 'Do penance for the Kingdom of God is at hand and be baptized every one of you in the Name of God the

Father and of the Son and of the Holy Ghost.' For many
months he preached to them at great length and with marvellous eloquence on the wondrous doings of the Lord in the
face of idolatry from the beginning of the world. He traced
these dealings for them in order right up to the day of judgement when eternal punishment is prepared for the wicked
and life everlasting for the elect. Then our holy bishop, God's
apostle and evangelist, found favour in the king's sight and,
as St Paul puts it, the great gate of the faith was laid open.
Hosts of pagans, some freely and some at the king's command, left their idolatry and acknowledged the Almighty
God, and many thousands were baptized in one day, as once
they were by the apostle Peter. The king, whom God had
filled with a spirit of gentle piety, gave up his own estate to
Wilfrid for an episcopal seat to which he later added about
nine thousand acres of land in Selsey. This he did out of
gratitude to the evangelist who had laid open by baptism the
gate of eternal life to him and all his subjects. Wilfrid gathered the brethren together and founded a community there in
retreat from the world. His followers have it to the present day.

## CHAPTER 42

### Ceadwalla becomes king

In those days when through our bishop's efforts the Church
of God was wonderfully increasing day by day and his own
fame was most gloriously shining forth, an exile of noble
birth came to him from the desert places of the Weald. His
name was Ceadwalla. He earnestly sought our father's friendship, vowing that if Wilfrid would be his spiritual father and
loyal helper he in turn would be an obedient son. This com-
pact, which they called God to witness, was faithfully fulfilled. Our holy bishop helped and supported Ceadwalla in all
kinds of ways through his many difficulties until at last he
was in a strong enough position to quell his enemies and
establish his sway over the whole area of West Saxony. Wilfrid was then converting the heathens of South Saxony and
glorifying the name of God by his labours. Ceadwalla sent

for him immediately, humbly summoning to his side the man he venerated as a father and loved above all others, and at once made him supreme counsellor over the whole kingdom; just as Pharaoh in the words of the prophet constituted Joseph on his release from prison 'master of his house so that he might impart wisdom'.

Thus God exalted our bishop through Ceadwalla's victory and Ceadwalla himself magnificently honoured his father with extensive lands and other gifts both out of natural affection and for the love of God. This new king steadfastly defended his country, preserving it from all harm by peace treaty and by the sword's edge.

## CHAPTER 43

ABOUT this time Archbishop Theodore was troubled with pangs of conscience and decided to honour the injunctions of the Roman See to which he owed his own appointment. So after his long delay during Wilfrid's impoverished exile he now made hasty overtures of friendship. By this time Theodore was well advanced in years and nearly always in bad health. He invited Wilfrid and Bishop Erconwald to London. In their presence he gave a frank account of his whole life and made his confession to God.

'What troubles me most,' he said, 'is the ill I did your lordship in consenting to the kings' action when they stripped you of all your goods and sent you into bitter exile to your own harm and the detriment of your people. Before God and St Peter I confess this sin. And now, my fellow bishops, I call you to witness that to make up for my fault I will do everything in my power to restore my royal friends and their noblemen to your friendship, whether they will or no. God has revealed to me that this coming year will be my last. I therefore implore you by God and St Peter not to go against my wish which is that you should succeed me as archbishop. Here and now I appoint you my heir, for of all your race you are the wisest and most learned in the canon law of the Holy See.'

Wilfrid replied: 'God and St Peter forgive you for all the opposition you stirred up against me. Now that you have made your confession I am your friend for ever and I shall pray for you. Only first send messengers to all your friends with letters to let them know that we are reconciled in the Lord and that, since my property was formerly confiscated without just cause, they are now to restore at least part of my goods. Later, God willing, the question of a worthy candidate for the archbishopric can be discussed in council.'

After this pact of true peace Theodore sent word to Aldfrith begging him, for the fear of God and out of respect for the Holy See's commands, to be reconciled to Wilfrid by peace treaty, for thus many would be saved, including King Ecgfrith, the principal cause of his poverty and exile. The archbishop did not confine himself to this one act but strove to make friends of all Wilfrid's former enemies. He wrote to the holy virgin, Abbess Aelfflaed, urging her to have no hesitation in obeying the Holy See and making friends with Wilfrid. Aethilred, King of Mercia, was requested, as he loved Christ and his own soul, to follow his former intention and renew relations with Wilfrid. Here is the text of the letter: 'To the most glorious, most excellent King Aethilred of the Mercians, Theodore, by God's grace archbishop, sends every grace and blessing in the Lord. Dearest son, may your wondrous holiness know that I am now at peace with Bishop Wilfrid. I urge you, beloved son, and charge you by the love of Christ, to do your utmost, as long as you live, to help this devoted servant of God, as you always used to in time past; and now especially, since for a long time now, while bereft of his own goods, he has been labouring among the pagans for the service of the Lord. Therefore I, Theodore, a humble bishop, now in my declining years, put this suggestion to your beatitude. It is no more than what Rome recommended. For this man Wilfrid does indeed possess his soul in patience, as the scripture says, imitating the meekness of his Master, Our Lord and Saviour, and humbly awaiting the redress of wrongs unjustly inflicted on him. If I have found favour in your sight, come, despite the discouraging length of the journey, and let me see your joyful face and let me bless you before I die. Now, my son, do as I ask concerning this most saintly man and your charity will stand you in good stead in the world to come. Go in peace; live with Christ; dwell in the Lord; and the Lord be with you.'

What more is there to say? King Aethilred, on account of those blessed pontiffs Agatho, Benedict, and Sergius – successors each in turn to the dignity of Peter – received our bishop in fulfilment of the canonical injunctions and did so most gladly. Many monasteries were returned to him and lands which he had possessed in his own right. Aethilred treated him with the deepest respect and remained his faithful friend for ever.

## CHAPTER 44

### *King Aldfrith receives our bishop*

MANY years had rolled by; our leader was living in honourable exile and his monks, scattered throughout the whole of Britain, were mourning under the yoke of masters not their own and praying for release. Then at last news came of a woeful disaster, a battle against the Picts, in which King Ecgfrith of Northumbria and the flower of his army had been mown down. Aldfrith, his successor, proved to be a wise ruler. In the second year of his reign he respectfully called Wilfrid back from exile, in obedience to Theodore. First of all he granted him the monastery at Hexham with all the possessions belonging to it and after a while, carrying out the command of Pope Agatho and the synod, he restored to him the see of York and the abbacy of Ripon together with their revenues, having driven out the usurping bishops. Like St John the Evangelist on his return to Ephesus, Wilfrid possessed them in security to the delight of his subjects, but only for five years.

## CHAPTER 45

### *Enmity is stirred up between Wilfrid and Aldfrith*

THOSE whose delight it is to stir up forgotten quarrels aroused themselves from their torpor and began disturbing the tenor of life which had up till then remained happily serene. They applied themselves to their envious designs until the storm clouds hovered and the brand of dissension was lighted afresh. For a while all would be peace between the wise King Aldfrith and our holy bishop, and a happier state of affairs could hardly be imagined. Then spite would boil up again and the situation would be reversed. And so they continued for years, in and out of friendship with each other, till finally their quarrels came to a head and the king banished Wilfrid from Northumbria. The principal cause of dissension was of long standing, namely the unjust removal of land and possessions from the Church of St Peter. The second was the making of the same monastery, which had been given to us as our own property, into an episcopal see. This entailed loss of rights that had been granted by Pope Agatho and confirmed by five kings. The third was Aldfrith's insistence on obedience to Theodore's edicts – not to those issued when he first took office nor those at the end of his reign whereby he had called all the churches to peace and concord in obedience to the canons, but only those from the middle period when all the trouble had started. Wilfrid refused to submit and betook himself to his friend the king of Mercia. Aethilred welcomed him with great honour out of reverence for the Apostolic See, so Wilfrid dwelt on there under his and God's protection and was held in high respect by the people of the diocese. It was the diocese the most reverend Bishop Sexwulf had ruled until his death.

## CHAPTER 46

### *The council at Austerfield**

So during the reign of Aldfrith a synod was held at Auster-field at which Archbishop Berhtwald and nearly all the bishops were present. They sent a deputation to Wilfrid ask-ing him very civilly to attend, on the assurance that with regard to his previous ill-treatment the statutes would now be honoured, so long as he did not refuse to come. Need I

* Near Bawtry, Yorkshire.

say more? Once he had arrived events turned out quite differently from what had been promised. Tremendous disputes and altercations broke out, fomented in the main by the avarice of some of the bishops. The peace of the Church was the last thing they wanted. They brought out all sorts of false objections, none of which was true, and in addition insisted that our holy bishop be judged according to Theodore's decrees. When Wilfrid realized the turn their arguments were taking he said that he was willing to obey in every respect, provided their decrees accorded with canon law. He went on to rebuke them at length for their contumacy, not mincing his words. For twenty-two years, he said, they had shamelessly opposed the authority of the pope. How, he asked them, could they have the effrontery to set at nought the apostolic decrees sent to Britain for the good of men's souls by three successive pontiffs, Agatho, Benedict, and Sergius, and choose rather to cling to the edicts of Archbishop Theodore, decisions made in the thick of the fray?

## CHAPTER 47

### *He discovers their trap*

IN the meantime, while they were attempting to draw up some kind of formal reply, one of the king's officers stole out of the king's tent and came to our bishop. Wilfrid had taken him in as a helpless infant, brought him up from the cradle in fact; consequently the man was greatly devoted to him. He came in disguise, mingling with the crowd, and explained that the bishops' decision was a trap.

'They are trying to trick you completely by getting you to sign their decision at the outset, so that afterwards you will be bound by whatever they think fit to stipulate. Your hands will then be tied; you will be powerless to alter a single clause. The upshot of the transaction will be that every single parcel of land you are known to possess in Northumbria, whether belonging to the diocese or the monasteries or coming to you in any other way, will be taken from you. You will be forced to surrender to the archbishop everything you have gained in Mercia from King Aethilred. Berhtwald will then give it to whom he pleases. Finally, you will find that your own signature has condemned you to degradation from the office of bishop.'

Having given his warning, the officer returned by stealth. Our holy bishop, being a man of great strength of character, thought the matter over and was much more wary of signing anything after that. The synod demanded an immediate reply, even threatening that if an answer were not forthcoming he might well find himself sentenced and condemned. His reply was: 'First let me hear the archbishop's decision; if it agrees with the rules laid down by the holy fathers, then I will embrace it with all my heart.'

In the end the synod could no longer conceal its plan. Its motives had been publicly known for some time. They openly declared that it was their wish to strip Wilfrid of all he possessed so that he would not be able to call the smallest cottage his own in either Northumbria or Mercia. The ruthlessness of the decision, for which the king and archbishop were responsible, shocked even Wilfrid's enemies. They cried out against the wickedness of leaving completely penniless a man famous throughout the whole country and especially as no capital offence could be brought against him. So they hit upon a slightly more humane design. Wilfrid would be allowed to keep the monastery at Ripon which he himself had built and dedicated to St Peter, with all its lands and possessions, and the privileges granted to the abbot and community would devolve on him. But the grant was made only on condition that he signed a solemn promise to the effect that he would stay there quietly and never leave the monastery bounds without royal consent, nor exercise his priestly office in any way at all, and finally that he would voluntarily lay down his rank. Thus they tried to force him to promise his own degradation on oath.

Wilfrid replied in steady fearless tones:

'Why are you trying to bring me to so sad a plight as to have me make my own signature an instrument of self-destruction? I have been a bishop now for nearly forty years and though unworthy of that rank I am completely innocent

of crime; yet you would have me drag down my own name
and make it a scandal to all who hear it. After the death of
those elders whom Pope Gregory sent to us was I not the first
to root out from the Church the foul weeds planted by the
Scots? Did I not convert the whole Northumbrian nation to
celebrating Easter at the proper time as the Holy See demanded, and to having the proper Roman tonsure in the form
of a crown instead of your old way of shaving the back of the
head from the top down? Did I not teach you to chant according to the practice of the early Church, with a two-part choir
each singing harmoniously and doing the responses and
chants together antiphonally? Did I not bring the monastic
life into line with the Rule of St Benedict never before introduced into these parts? And now, have I got to bring some
hurried sentence against myself, unconscious though I am of
any crime committed? With regard to this latest novelty of
yours whereby you seek to violate my very office, I appeal in
all confidence to the Holy See. Here and now I challenge anyone who presumes to degrade me to accompany me thither
to seek judgement. You ought to let the Roman officials, who
are no fools, know what charge you bring against me, before
I submit to you alone.'

To this the king and archbishop replied: 'Now at any rate
he is guilty. Let him stand condemned for preferring their
judgement to ours.'

The king added to the archbishop's proposal: 'If you want,
I can use my army to put pressure on him and force him,
this time without the slightest delay, to say how willing he
is to accept our decision.'

But here the other synodal bishops interrupted: 'We ought
to remember that he only came here on the promise of safe
conduct from us; otherwise he would never have ventured.
Let us all return home in peace.'

## CHAPTER 48

### *Wilfrid returns to Aethilred*

AFTER these indecisive efforts the fruitless synod was dissolved by both sides and everyone went home. So, by God's protection, His servant was freed from the hands of his enemies and returned unharmed to the faithful King Aethilred. Wilfrid recounted the whole bitter attack made by the bishops in the face of his, Aethilred's, injunctions, and asked what sort of decrees he had made concerning the lands and privileges he had previously granted him. The king replied:

'I have no intention of adding trouble to trouble by taking away the livelihood of the monks of St Peter's Abbey. While I live, my former grant stands and on exactly the same conditions as, with God's blessing, have hitherto prevailed, until such time as I shall send either messengers or messages with you to Rome to have these urgent affairs settled. And may I find salvation in seeking to do right.'

This answer gave them both cause for rejoicing. Then they parted, each to his own home.

## CHAPTER 49

### *We are excommunicated*

WILFRID's enemies, not content with appropriating his possessions, declared that we and all who had dealings with us were no longer part of the body of the faithful. They even went so far in severing communion with us as to hold that if any of our priests or abbots should be invited to a meal by any of the 'faithful' and should bless the food on the table with the sign of the cross, then that food should be thrown away as though it were meat offered to idols and the dishes used by our men should be purified before being considered fit for use again.

## CHAPTER 50

### *His voyage to Rome*

W HEN we learned of the tragic calamity that had befallen
both ourselves and all the congregations attached to us, we
spent the time, until Bishop Wilfrid's party was ready to embark, in fasting and tears, praying and beseeching the Lord.
They set sail and, with God before to guide them, reached
the southern shores. Then, with the help of the holy apostles,
they made their way overland and reached Rome on foot. On
being presented at the papal court they went down on bended
knee and begged with all urgency that the Holy See should
receive the written account of the reason for their coming
and show its usual kindly indulgence by disregarding the
rusticity of style and lack of polish in the composition of the
document.

'We wish your Holiness to understand that we have not
come here to accuse anyone out of spite but simply to hear
whatever objections might be brought against us by our
opponents and, with the help of your clemency, to do our
best to refute them if false or admit them if true. Under the
protection of our Creator and with the help of the Prince of
the Apostles we have sought refuge in this most glorious see,
as though in our mother's lap and are completely prepared to
bow to your authority.'

Pope John gave our holy prelate and his venerable priests
and clergy a very warm welcome and provided free lodging
for them so that they could enjoy a few days' rest while awaiting a decision from the illustrious see of Rome. Archbishop
Berhtwald's representatives happened to arrive at the same
time as Wilfrid with written accusations and had begged a
hearing for their claims. The pope, therefore, called all his
fellow-bishops and clergy together to form a synod. Wilfrid
and his party were presented and the meeting began with a
reading of his petition. It ran as follows.

CHAPTER 51

*The text of the petition*

'To the Apostolic Lord and thrice-blessed universal father, Pope John, Wilfrid, a simple and humble servant of God's servants and a bishop, pays honour. I wish to make known to your Holiness the reasons why I have come a third time to the Holy See from the far ends of the earth to seek help in your presence. They are these: First I hope to hear you confirm and corroborate all those most just and merciful decrees of your blessed predecessor Pope Agatho. Such a hope is grounded both on the belief that your action would bring about the salvation of many souls and on the fact of the undivided solidarity of judgement in the line of the popes. Secondly I would have your Holiness understand that we are only too ready to submit humbly to your commands. I have been led to make this appeal by the recent disturbances in Britain caused by that faction which, in contravention of Pope Agatho's decrees, have robbed me of my bishopric, monasteries, land, and everything I possessed. I adjured my assailants by the Most High God and by St Peter to follow the procedure laid down by Pope Sergius if they had anything to charge me with, and to accompany me hither to be judged in your presence. In view of the patent urgency of my claims I have been at pains to have a list of my humble petitions delivered to your august Eminence, in addition to which I now make bold to assail your ears with the request that your benign clemency may see fit to confirm with abounding holy benevolence all those good and just decrees made so unanimously on my poor behalf by your illustrious predecessors, the Apostolic Lords St Agatho, blessed Sergius, and the glorious Pope Benedict. Moreover I myself and my companions here humbly beg you from the bottom of our hearts, should anyone appear with charges against us, to use your inflexible authority to bid him come forward and make them openly in your presence. If even the smallest accusation holds water we will gladly submit to your judgement; if, however, my opponents do not scruple to foist a pack of lies on your Holiness, backed up with false documentation, then please give us leave to clear ourselves in person. I also earnestly ask your Holiness to send orders to King Aethilred of Mercia regarding my well-being, repeating what was laid down by your three predecessors – that no one is to presume, either through foul greed or envy, to lay hands on those monasteries or their lands which Aethilred or his brother Wulfhere or anybody else may have given me for their souls' salvation. I urge you to give your orders the same force of authority as those of your forerunners. Furthermore, and this is most important, I implore you to be so kind as to advise King Aldfrith of Northumbria, in very quiet diplomatic tones, to carry out all the decrees of Pope Agatho and the synod. But if this should go against the grain with him, because of my part in the business, then use your own judgement in deciding who is best fitted to govern the see of York and all its numerous monasteries – except the houses of Hexham and Ripon which Pope Agatho included under one and the same privilege. Ask that they be restored to us with all their lands and possessions.

'To all these partitions I add this : I always show proper respect and fraternal charity towards Archbishop Berhtwald and I shall continue to do so. Only let him carry out those firmly established decrees made on behalf of my poor self by Agatho and his successors.'

CHAPTER 52

*Pope John declares that the writings of his predecessors are to be examined*

AFTER the full text of our petition had been read out and given a hearing by the illustrious assembly, we were given leave to retire to our lodgings and the envoys of Archbishop Berhtwald were called in to present their documents. The accusations they brought against Wilfrid were many and serious. The court, therefore, promised that both parties would be called at some future date and that each count would be thoroughly examined in turn. It then bade them withdraw and Pope John addressed his fellow-bishops.

'Members of this holy synod, it is our duty first of all to go through the canons of our holy predecessors, and examine the documents treating of these injuries and wrongs sent by either party up to now. We must bear in mind and carefully weigh what blessed Agatho and Benedict and my holy predecessor Sergius thought of the matter, and what orders they gave the kings and archbishops. After that, with the help of God and the Prince of the Apostles, we shall be in a better position to stamp out falsehood and perceive the light of truth when we have both sides before us in the presence of our brethren contesting against each other. We shall follow the canons and judge according to the rules laid down by our predecessors.'

The whole synod was pleased with this plan and proceeded to put it into action.

CHAPTER 53

So on the day appointed the most blessed John, Bishop of the Apostolic See, sitting in council with his right reverend bishops, ordered representatives of each side, both accusers and accused, to present themselves before the holy gathering. This was no sooner said than done. Our holy Bishop Wilfrid with his venerable priests and deacons came in as humble suppliants. They greeted the honourable assembly and promised to obey and carry out their decision with the greatest good-will. The archbishop's men were also present. They were given time to speak and told that they could choose any one heading from their list of accusations and speak on that and then proceed in order to the other points listed for discussion. They answered:

'This is our main charge, namely that Bishop Wilfrid here present contumaciously despised and rejected before our synod the statutes of Berhtwald, Archbishop of the Kentish

Church and of all Britain and a man who was sent to us by the Apostolic See itself. We have given our view. Now let us hear the defence.'

St Wilfrid, bent under the weight of an honourable old age, rose, surrounded by his brethren, in the sight of the whole gathering.

'I speak as humble suppliant to your most excellent Holiness, asking you to condescend to hear from my own lips a true account of the actions of my unworthy self. I was indeed present at the council with my abbots, priests, and deacons, for they sent one of the bishops to ask me in the name of the king and the archbishop whether or not I was prepared to submit to the archbishop's judgement alone and zealously carry out his decisions. I answered thus: "We must be informed of the broad outlines of these decisions before we can commit ourselves one way or another." The bishop said he himself had not known and that the archbishop had declared that he would by no means let any of our party know what he had resolved upon until we had given a written promise before the synod to submit to his judgement in every single matter, and not to deviate from it one step either to left or right. "I have never in my life heard of so rigid and narrow a constraint", I replied. "I am to bind myself on oath to carry out a whole mass of decrees, no matter how impossible they may prove to be, without knowing the terms of even one of them." None the less I promised the synod my wholehearted assent to everything laid down by the archbishop, as long as it tallied with the rules and statutes of the holy fathers and with the canonical definitions and was not in conflict with the synods of St Agatho and his orthodox successors.'

After offering this defence our holy bishop was silent.

The synod fathers continued: 'Bishop Wilfrid, God's beloved, has set forth in accordance with the canons, the defence under which he seeks to shelter.'

Then they began speaking in Greek and smiled to themselves, and had a long discussion that they kept concealed from us and finally addressed our accusers.

'You are not ignorant, dear brethren, of the canonical prescription which reads: "When a number of charges are brought against clerics, if the first one cannot be proved the prosecution is not to proceed to the rest." Nevertheless, out of respect for the archbishop whom we ourselves sent to Britain and in reverence to this most blessed Bishop Wilfrid – who has been so long fraudulently despoiled – we, asking God and St Peter to reveal the truth of the matter, shall willingly put ourselves out and spend weeks and months sifting every charge, for we intend to settle the case once and for all.'

After that the synod gave our bishop and his brethren, for whom the joy of victory had already begun, permission to return to their lodgings. There they set about preparing for the skirmishes to come. Their opponents, on the other hand, returned home in confusion at the result of this first hearing. Several months later their pack of lies was blown away by the blast of wisdom, and with the help of God and St Peter the truth shone clearly forth, showing our holy pontiff completely and utterly free from anything deserving of degradation : for after seventy sessions of the council over a period of four months, in which he was refined in a veritable furnace of cross-examination, he was acquitted. The Holy See came to his aid in the following way : at Easter, on the third day of the feast, a synod consisting of one hundred and twenty-five orthodox bishops under Pope Agatho was held to root out heretical corruption. Each of the bishops witnessed to the true faith on behalf of his province and city and then confirmed the testimony with his signature. This document was read out in a loud voice before all the people, as is the custom in Rome, and in it, among other items, occurred the following passage :

'Wilfrid, Bishop of the city of York, having appealed to the Apostolic See and having been cleared by the same authority of certain definite and indefinite charges, did, together with one hundred and twenty-five of his fellow-bishops in this synod and judgement seat, confess the true and Catholic faith on behalf of all the northern part of Britain and Ireland and the islands inhabited by the Angles, Britons, Picts, and Scots, and did corroborate the same with his signature.'

When they heard this all the wise citizens of Rome were

amazed. Then Boniface and Sizentius and some others who remembered him from Pope Agatho's time spoke up.

'This Bishop Wilfrid,' they said, 'is the one whom blessed Agatho sent home cleared, by apostolic authority, of every charge levelled against him; but now, alas, the malice of trouble-makers has sent him wandering from his own see. He has been a bishop now for forty years and more, yet those false accusers still do not think shame to forge documents against the venerable old man and his companions. These scoundrels, one a deacon and the rest mere laymen without the least ecclesiastical rank or dignity, have even had the temerity to arraign His Lordship before the Holy See. They deserve the harshest punishment – let them be thrown into the deepest dungeons to waste away till death.'

The citizens of Rome said they had spoken the truth. Then the pope spoke.

'We have examined the case of blessed Bishop Wilfrid, whom God loves, in numerous sessions of this council, and we can find nothing against him. Therefore, by the authority of St Peter, Prince of the Apostles, in whom resides the power of binding or loosing from secret sins, we declare him acquitted. Moreover, unworthy though we be, we have decided, with the consent of the whole synod, to confirm whatever Agatho, Benedict, and Sergius, bishops of the holy city, decided on his behalf and delivered in writing by Wilfrid's own hand to the kings and archbishop.'

Here follows the text of the decree.

## CHAPTER 54

'Pope John to their most noble majesties, Aethilred King of Mercia and Aldfrith, King of Deira. We fully recognize your zeal for the faith which you received when God illumined your hearts through the preaching of the Prince of the Apostles and which you firmly hold; and we rejoice in the great increase of religion among you – may greater growth increase our joy! But the news of this tangle of dissension saddens not only ourselves but also our fellow-clergy and indeed the whole Church. The matter must now be completely disentangled, with God's help, so that you yourselves, in the presence of the Lord and Judge of all, may stand out not as despisers but as the upholders of the pontifical decrees and as our obedient sons. Some time ago, during the pontificate of Pope Agatho of blessed memory, Bishop Wilfrid came in person with an appeal to the Apostolic See. His adversaries, representatives of the holy Abbess Hilda and of Theodore of hallowed memory, archbishop of the Kentish nation by mandate of this same see, were present too. An assembly was then convened of bishops of various provinces who held a formal inquiry into the arguments of either side and decided accordingly. And this decision our holy predecessors have confirmed. Bishop Theodore is not known to have contravened this nor to have made any further accusation; on the contrary, it is quite clear from his own words that he complied. Consequently we must have recourse to God's aid to see that dissension does not continue to smoulder in one part of the Church, while in every other province clergy and people are in perfect harmony. So much for the past. Regarding the present, we have taken measures to inform your renowned majesties that a delegation recently came to us from your own island of Britain to bring accusations against Bishop Wilfrid. He himself arrived shortly afterwards and rebutted the charges by turning them back upon the accusers themselves. We had the parties debate the matter for some days before an assembly of reverend priests and prelates. Every document, old or new, adduced by either side, all their verbal statements, together with any relevant matter we could find in our archives – all this has been most carefully sifted and the findings made known to us. However, the principal protagonists in the dispute, those who started it all, were not here; but it will be necessary for them to meet and confer before the affair can be concluded once and for all. Therefore we hereby order our most reverend brother Berhtwald, whom we ourselves on the authority of the Prince of the Apostles have confirmed in office as Archbishop of the Kentish

Church, to convoke a synod with Bishop Wilfrid and that, when this council has been properly constituted, he call Bishops Bosa and John to give evidence. He must hear each side and carefully weigh their claims, noting what can really be proved. If, in his opinion, the matter can be properly settled by the synod, then both ourselves and the rival factions will be satisfied. But if it turns out otherwise, he must give them formal warning in synod and admonish them privately and go over every single point at issue. They must come to Rome together and have the quarrel thrashed out in a fuller council so that a final decision may be reached on what has up to now eluded settlement. Then, by the grace of the Holy Spirit, those who have come in discord may perhaps be able to return in peace. Whoever puts off the journey or (and this we execrate) will not deign to come is to be informed that he is thereby removed from office. He must be expelled and the clergy and people of the district forbidden to receive him, for he who sets himself up against his Master is not to be counted among His ministers and disciples. Therefore, for the fear of God and out of reverence for the Christian faith and for that peace which Our Lord Jesus Christ gave to His followers, may your Royal and Christian Highnesses lend your assistance, so that these matters which with Christ's help we have so closely examined may now be happily concluded. Do so and your labours in the cause of religion will be rewarded by a peaceful reign under Christ's protection in this world and the blessed fellowship of His Eternal Kingdom in the next. Recall to mind, beloved sons, what Agatho and the bishops of the Roman Church after him have laid down on apostolic authority in this very question. For he who with rash temerity despises our commands, however high his rank may be, will not go unpunished by God and, being found guilty by Heaven, how can he escape without loss? God's grace keep your Highnesses forever safe.'

## CHAPTER 55

*Wilfrid is ordered to return home and brings*
*back the holy relics*

AFTER several months of almost daily examination and close
questioning Wilfrid emerged completely exonerated. His
case was won. His one wish now was to remain permanently
in the Holy City and there end his days, crucifying himself to
the world (as St Paul said) in his old age; but he had promised humble obedience to the pope and synod and they both
ordered him to leave for home. Now that his long period of
affliction had been brought to an end by complete acquittal
from every charge both particular and general, they bade him
return to present the findings in writing to the kings and
archbishops, to soothe his subjects' grief and give his friends
cause for rejoicing. Our holy bishop knew how to obey. He
went round the shrines of the saints with his companions
making a collection of relics, each labelled with the saint's
name, and he bought purple cloth and silk vestments to
decorate his churches. Then, with the blessing of the saints
upon him, he made his way homewards by paths rough and
smooth, over mountain and plain, till after a long journey he
reached the Kingdom of Gaul.

## CHAPTER 56

*Our patron falls sick and St Michael appears to him*

ON the way home our holy bishop became gravely ill. At
first he went along on horseback but later had to be carried
in a litter. His friends mourned and wept over his condition
and called upon God for aid. They brought him into Meaux
scarcely alive and were convinced he was dying, for he was
still breathing and warm to the touch but unconscious. Nothing had passed his lips for the last four days, but on the fifth
day, as dawn was breaking, an angel of the Lord in shining
raiment appeared to him. 'I am Michael, messenger of the

Most High God,' he announced. 'I have come to tell you that through the prayers of the ever-virgin Mary, Mother of God, and the tears of your followers, several years have been added to your life, as a sign of which your health will improve daily until you are completely well, you will reach your native land in safety, all your precious possessions will be restored to you and you will end your days in peace. I will visit you four years from now: be prepared. You have built churches in honour of St Peter and St Andrew but for the Blessed Mary, ever-virgin, who is interceding for you, you have built nothing. Rectify this omission by dedicating a church in her honour.' The angel of the Lord was taken up and disappeared from his sight. Our holy bishop arose as though he had just awoken and sat down with his friends who were weeping and chanting prayers for him.

'Where is our priest Acca?' he asked.

Acca was called in and rejoiced and thanked God with the rest of them at the sight of his master sitting up and talking. Wilfrid asked the brethren to withdraw and leave him alone with his faithful chaplain. He revealed the vision detail by detail. Acca, being a man of acute intelligence (he is now a bishop), at once recognized the parallel between this favour and that accorded Hezekiah, King of Judah, and thanked God accordingly. Wilfrid's life was spared at the intercession of the Mother of God and his own followers: Hezekiah's life was lengthened by fifteen years, five because of his father David, five through the prophet Isaiah's prayers in the temple, and five of his own goodness and because he had turned his face to the wall and wept.

## CHAPTER 57

### *The return crossing*

WHILE the brethren were rejoicing heartily at his recovery, our holy father washed his hands and face and took a little food and then like Jonathan 'his eyes were enlightened and he revived'. They set out a few days later when he was back to his full strength, reached and crossed the breadth of the ocean and found safe harbour, by God's help, on the coast of Kent. Wilfrid's messengers sought out Archbishop Berht-wald and conferred with him. Peaceful relations were restored. The papal brief commanding obedience terrified him, so in fear and trembling he promised to mitigate the harsh decrees passed long ago by his own synod – a promise which turned out to be completely genuine. Wilfrid progressed joyfully westwards to London accompanied by a whole cortège of his abbots and laden with presents. From there he went on to visit that faithful friend whose loyalty had never wavered, Aethilred, the former king of Mercia. He was received with all the usual honours; they kissed and embraced and Aethilred was so overcome with joy that he could not restrain himself. He simply burst into tears. Wilfrid then formally greeted him in the name of the Holy See and respectfully presented the text of the papal bull properly stamped and sealed. As soon as the document had been opened and read, Aethilred prostrated himself on the ground in token of obedience.

'Never in all my life shall I think lightly of one jot or tittle of this decree, nor shall I countenance those who do so. I shall do all in my power to enforce it.'

This was no idle promise. Aethilred's goodness will be rewarded above.

Not content with this, he summoned Coenred, whom he had appointed his heir, and made him swear, out of the love he bore him and in God's name, to uphold the precepts of the Holy See. This Coenred willingly promised.

## CHAPTER 58

### *King Aldfrith despises him and meets his doom*

SHORTLY afterwards, on Aethilred's advice, Wilfrid sent a delegation to King Aldfrith of Northumbria. This task he entrusted to two men whom he knew well, Badwini, a priest and abbot, and Alfrith. They spoke as follows:

'Our holy bishop sends friendly greetings and begs permission to come in person to present the greetings of the Holy

See together with its authoritative answer to his appeal.'

The king's immediate reply was not at all harsh. He merely arranged the date for a future meeting at which, he promised, they would receive an answer. Badwini and Alfrith duly presented themselves on the appointed day and asked what he had decided. He said what his counsellors had persuaded him to say.

'My friends, I respect you – so highly indeed that you have only to ask for whatever you want and you shall have it. But pester me no more with this business of your master Wilfrid. My kingly predecessors, the archbishop, and their counsellors arrived at a certain decision in which I myself, Archbishop Berhtwald and almost the entire body of British bishops later concurred. It still stands. As long as I live no documents you may bring forward as emanating from the Holy See will make me change.'

But he later repented and did change his mind – completely.


CHAPTER 59


THEY had no further interview, but left at once to bring Wilfrid the sad news. And now, just as the pope had promised, divine vengeance did not tarry. Aldfrith soon had to grapple with a severe illness. He at once came to his senses, realized that he had been stricken down by the power of the apostles for his defiance of Rome, and repented.

'If only Wilfrid could be persuaded to come to me now,' he lamented, 'I would quickly make amends.'

There and then he vowed to God and St Peter that if he were spared to rise from his bed he would carry out the pope's commands, let Wilfrid have his way and put everything in order.

'But if by God's will I should die, I bid my successor, whoever he may be, to come to terms with Wilfrid for the good of his soul and my own.'

This verbatim account was given us by trustworthy witnesses among whom were Abbess Aelffled, herself a king's daughter, and Abbess Aethilberg. Many others have confirmed it. But the king's illness gained the upper hand; he lay speechless for five days, then died. Eadwulf succeeded him for a short while. Our holy bishop, who was at Ripon with Eadwulf's son, sent messengers to him as a friend – only to be answered with extreme harshness, for the deep-rooted malice of Eadwulf's counsellors had turned him against Wilfrid. This was the reply :

'I swear on my life that if you are not out of my kingdom within six days, you and any of your companions I can find shall perish.'

Shortly afterwards a conspiracy was hatched against the king and he was driven out after a mere two months' reign. The boy Osred, Aldfrith's son, took his place and became our bishop's adopted son.

CHAPTER 60

In the first year of Osred's reign Berhtwald, Archbishop of Canterbury and primate of nearly the whole of Britain, came up from the south to invite the king of the northern regions together with all his bishops, abbots, and chief men of rank in the kingdom to settle Wilfrid's case in synod by the east bank of the Nidd.* Abbess Aelffled, the best of advisers and a constant source of strength to the whole province, was with them. Archbishop Berhtwald and Wilfrid both arrived on the same day. The whole company took their seats and Berht-wald opened the proceedings.

'Let us ask Our Lord Jesus Christ,' he began, 'to grant us peace and concord through His Holy Spirit. I have with me documents sent by the Holy See to my unworthy self and Bishop Wilfrid has others that he brought from Rome. We humbly ask your reverences' leave to read them out.'

Permission was granted and each volume was read out from beginning to end. After the reading there was complete silence. Then Berhtfrith, a nobleman, second in rank only to the king, addressed the archbishop :

* Exact site not known.

'Those of us who could not manage to follow the reading would be grateful if you would explain just what the Holy See means.'

The archbishop replied:

'The papal pronouncements are couched in obscure and roundabout terms but one single lesson emerges from both. Briefly it is this: The Holy See, by the power of loosing and binding first given to St Peter, and on its own authority, had decided that in my unworthy presence and before the whole synod, you prelates of the churches of this province must, as you value your salvation, put aside all long-standing enmity and be reconciled to Wilfrid once and for all. The Apostolic See leaves two ways open to you, one of which you must choose: either to live in full and perfect harmony with Wilfrid and give him back all his former jurisdiction – the extent of which will be determined by myself and certain prudent advisers – or, if you are unwilling to take the better course, then you must all go to Rome and have your quarrels thrashed out before a higher court. Whosoever rejects both courses (God forbid that anyone should!), whether he be king or commoner, is to be excommunicated from the Body and Blood of Christ. Should any bishop or priest act like this (which would be even fouler – in fact I shudder to think of it) he is to be degraded from holy orders. That is the gist of the letters.'

But the bishops did not give way.

'Who can alter,' they claimed, 'the decrees passed by King Ecgfrith and Archbishop Theodore whom the pope sent out here to us, decisions which we, the bishops of nearly the whole of Britain, later confirmed with King Aldfrith in your Grace's own most excellent presence at Austerfield?'

Then the holy Abbess Aelffled rose and spoke these inspired words:

'Let me tell you, truly and in Christ's name, what King Aldfrith's last will and testament, the one he made on his deathbed, really was. He made a vow to God and St Peter in the following terms: "If I live I promise to fulfil all those judgements of the Apostolic See in regard to Wilfrid which formerly I had refused even to hear. If I die bid my son and heir, for the good of my soul, do the same." '

When she had finished, Berhtfrith spoke.

'The king and his earls will that the command of the Holy See and King Aldfrith's instructions be obeyed to the last detail. For when we were besieged at Bamburgh, surrounded by enemies on all sides and forced to take refuge in a narrow rocky cleft, we held a discussion on this very subject and vowed that if God granted our royal boy his father's kingdom, we would carry out the apostolic injunctions concerning Bishop Wilfrid. No sooner had we made this vow than the enemy completely changed their minds. They came rushing up to make friends with us. The gates were opened, we came out into the open air, hostilities were over and the kingdom ours.'

At this the bishops went to one side and began talking among themselves. The archbishop gave them his advice and Abbess Aelffled gave them hers. The parley ended with the decision, in which they were joined by king and counsellors, to make an unconditional peace pact with Wilfrid. And they kept it till their lives' end. He got back the two best monasteries, Ripon and Hexham, with all their revenues. Then all the bishops embraced each other and joined together in the Breaking of Bread. They thanked God for all these wonderful blessings and set off home. And Christ's peace went with them.

CHAPTER 61

'GOD is wondrous in his saints,' says the Psalmist and indeed he is, for out of the love He bears the whole Church he cleansed the bishops' hearts of enmity and crowned them with peace. What a source of blessing the settlement was to both parties! Those who, after so long a tenure of Wilfrid's possessions gave them up to make amends before his death, brought down Christ's peace upon themselves; while to us their action brought new hope and restored to us all the joys of our old way of life. We had been scattered abroad as exiles in various parts of the country under strange masters.

Now our misery was over and we could again enjoy community life under our beloved superior and live in peace with all who were reconciled to him.

## CHAPTER 62

BUT in this world no joy comes to us unmixed with sorrow and everything is by nature mortal. Our holy bishop was on his way to Hexham when the time foretold by the Archangel Michael came round. He fell suddenly ill with the same complaint that had stricken him at Meaux, only this time the attack was worse. We, the members of his household, overwhelmed with anguish, rushed to the armoury of prayer. We chanted and prayed day and night without ceasing, imploring God to prolong his life so that at least he might have time to speak to us and appoint abbots to his monasteries and divide up his possessions lest we should be left like orphans without a superior. The news of this calamity spread quickly. All his abbots and hermits came hastening in from far and wide. They even travelled on through the night in the hope of seeing him alive and refused to be turned back by rumours of his death. We were sure he would die before they arrived, but were proved wrong. Entering the house they all knelt down with one accord, beseeching the Lord to remember His promise : 'When two or three are gathered together in My Name, there am I in the midst of them', and not to take their bishop just yet. Their prayer was heard. He was given time to arrange everything that had not yet been put in order, namely to lay down the rule of life for the various houses and appoint superiors and share out his goods as he thought fit between God and man, that is to allot some for sacred, some for profane use. His reason, memory, and power of speech all came back to him; indeed the sickness left him as sleep goes on waking. We were overjoyed at this complete recovery, and having thanked God for it each went off on his own way.

## CHAPTER 63

To the great joy of his subjects our saintly master lived to enjoy another eighteen months of perfect tranquillity. He spent the time putting to rights all those affairs that had badly needed settling. Shortly before that memorable final day he summoned two of his abbots and six of his most faithful friends to Ripon. He bade the treasurer open the diocesan coffers and set out all the gold, silver, and precious stones in front of them in four separate piles. Wilfrid himself decided into which pile each object should go. The official quickly laid out the treasure and then Wilfrid addressed his trusty witnesses:

'Dearly beloved, I would have you know that it has long been my intention, God willing, to return to Rome to end my days in the See which has so often solved my difficulties for me. I had thought to take one of these four piles with me as an offering to the churches, particularly to the church dedicated to the Mother of the Lord and to offer gifts to St Paul's for the welfare of my soul. But, as happens to old people, God has disposed otherwise. Death is overtaking me here. So I am now giving orders to you, my faithful companions, to send messengers with the treasure to the churches I have just mentioned. Of the three remaining parts one is to be given to the poor of my diocese for the repose of my soul, the second is to go to the abbots of Hexham and Ripon so that they might have something in hand wherewith to secure the favour of the kings and bishops, the third is for those who laboured with me in my long exile and whom I have not already rewarded with lands or estates. Share it out between them according to their needs so that they will be able to maintain themselves after I am gone.'

He paused a while, then continued.

'Take note, brethren, that I appoint the priest Tatberht here present, as abbot of Ripon. He is my kinsman and has been my inseparable companion up to now. While I live we will rule jointly; when I die he will be in sole command. I want you to be quite clear on that point. I am making these decrees now so that, when the Archangel Michael comes to fetch me, he may find me prepared. For the signs of death are crowding thick about me.'

## CHAPTER 64

THE meeting over, Wilfrid had a bell rung to assemble the whole community.

'Our well-beloved brother Caelin,' he began, 'has for a long time now been our leader in the observance of the Rule. He has worked extremely hard in God's service and now wants to go back to his former way of life in the wild parts of the country to serve God only by giving himself up to solitary contemplation. I will deny his wish no longer.

'Our abbots Tibba and Ebba are here from King Coelred of Mercia to ask me to go and confer with him and they have persuaded me to agree to this for the sake of the monasteries we have in that kingdom. Coelred has promised to make me his director and to follow my judgement in regulating the whole course of his life.

'I urge you to keep the rule faithfully till, if God wills it, I return. Should he will otherwise and my many infirmities overtake me, then I bid you to accept as abbot whomever my witnesses here – Abbots Tibba and Ebba, the priest Tatberht and Hathufrith and Master Alnhfrith – shall come and declare to you. The obedience you promised to God and myself and which you have hitherto rendered, you shall give to him.'

They knelt down weeping, heads bowed to the ground, and promised to fulfil all his commands; and as they prostrated themselves in prayer our holy bishop gave his blessing and commended them to God. The community never saw him again.

## CHAPTER 65

ST WILFRID set off for the south and the goodwill of the whole Northumbrian people, high and low, went with him. His abbots in Mercia were overjoyed to see him. He went round the abbeys as one who has foreseen his end and is sharing out his property among his heirs. His generosity was truly heart-warming. Every community was provided for according to its needs; some got grants of land to increase their revenues, the rest were left a legacy. To a few of the abbots he confided the full details of his will. At the end of the round his company came to the monastery at Oundle where Wilfrid had once dedicated a church to St Andrew, and here he was twice overcome by sudden illness. He knew his end was nigh and contented himself with exhorting them to follow all the good advice he had previously given. (Sometime before this, as though he knew he was soon to die, he had given his kinsman Tatberht a full account of his life one day when they were out riding.) He mentioned all the grants of land he had made to his abbots and which he now left them in his will. Hexham Abbey he gave to Acca, who afterwards succeeded him in the see. He talked a little while and blessed them, just as Jacob blessed his sons, then, quietly, without any fuss or complaint, leaned back on the pillow and rested. The brethren chanted round the bed day and night, weeping as they sang. When they came to the verse of Psalm 103 which runs 'Send forth Thy Spirit and they shall be created, and Thou shalt renew the face of the earth,' our bishop breathed his last. And the brethren heard, to their amazement, a sound in the air like a flight of birds approaching. This fact is attested to by crowds of witnesses. Wilfrid's nominee, Acca, was accepted as abbot in his place. The depth of the love he bore his father in God can be seen in the numerous practices he instituted in his honour. Acca himself celebrated a private mass daily for the repose of his soul and had every Thursday, the day of his death, kept as a feast just like Sunday. He decided to mark every anniversary of the death by giving a tenth part of all his herds and flocks to the poor – all this over and above the charity he distributed every day for the repose of his master's soul and the welfare of his own, always in Wilfrid's name.

CHAPTER 66

WE looked on our holy bishop as a great man and a faithful servant of Christ, but our Lord, by the miracles worked on his behalf, made it known that he was no less than a saint living with Him in glory. It happened one day that all the abbots came to Oundle to carry away the body in a carriage. Some of them wanted to wash the corpse and have it decently vested (as indeed was only right and proper) and obtained permission to do so. Abbot Bacula spread out his robe on the ground and the brethren laid the body on it. After the washing and vesting, which the abbots themselves performed, it was taken with great reverence to the place appointed. And, lo, once again from over the monastery came the sound of birds alighting and taking off with a gentle, almost musical flapping of wings. The wiser members of the community were convinced that Michael had come with his choirs of angels to lead our bishop's soul to Paradise. The washing had been done outside the monastery buildings in a tent put up for the purpose and the water had been emptied out in the same place. The monks erected a cross to mark the spot and many miracles were later performed there. Our monks wrapped up the holy remains in linen, placed them in the carriage, and brought it to Ripon, chanting as they came. The community came out with the holy relics to honour the cortège and hardly any of them managed to fight back his tears. They found voice, nevertheless, to sing the hymns and canticles for the reception of the corpse and led it into the basilica he himself had built and dedicated to St Peter. There he was buried with all honour in the seventy-sixth year of his age and the fortieth of his episcopate. Who can tell how many bishops, priests, and deacons he had consecrated and ordained or count the churches he had dedicated during all those years? His glory shall endure for ever. After the funeral his worthy successor Tatberht was led in surrounded by all the other bishops.

The abbot who had given his cloak for Wilfrid to be laid out on told his servant lad to take it to Wilfrid's abbess, Cynithrith. It was rather dirty from being trodden on during the washing. Cynithrith's orders were to keep it just as it was, folded up, till the abbot should visit her. At first she did as she was bidden but after a while decided to have it washed. There was a poor nun in the convent who, like the mason in the gospel, had gone about for years with a withered hand. Hearing what the abbess was doing she came and knelt before her with tears in her eyes.

'In the name of the Lord Jesus Christ,' she begged, 'and by the soul of your dear bishop, let me bathe my shrivelled limb in the washing water. I have unshakeable faith in the power of this water, mixed as it is with the saint's sweat, to cure my crooked hand and withered arm.'

The abbess, being a pious woman, dared hardly refuse the sister. To show her faith she at once picked up the lifeless hand with her good one and plunged it into the warm soapy water and rubbed it with the cloak. And, lo and behold, the fingers straightened out, the hand regained its vitality, and she got back the use of her whole arm. Like Moerisa, the woman in the gospel who was cured of an issue of blood by touching the hem of Christ's garment, her faith had made her whole, and like her prototype she gave thanks to God, praising Him for His wonderful works.

### CHAPTER 67

On another occasion the Lord made it clear that our great and worthy bishop was a saint. There was a group of exiles, noblemen too, going round with an armed band, ravaging the countryside out of revenge. They wantonly set fire to the monastery at Oundle where Wilfrid had been called to his fathers. They did their utmost with torches and firebrands to raze it to the ground, and succeeded – except for the room where the saint had died. Here the torches, instead of setting ablaze, guttered out. Thinking that the wet thatch on the roof might have damped them out, one of the marauders pushed his way into the room to light the dry straw inside. There within stood a young man in white holding a golden cross. The man rushed out in terror yelling:

'Quick, away from here! An angel of the Lord is protecting the place.'

They quickly retreated.

There is another fact connected with the raid, which is very well vouched for. One side of the great thorn hedge round the monastery was set alight, and the flames raced along it burning all before them till they came to the place where the cross was standing, and then suddenly died out. The fire had also crept round the other side of the buildings along the parched hedge. When it reached where the corner of Wilfrid's room jutted out, the flames died away. That was the only bit of hedge saved.

God's punishment soon lighted on the evil-doers. Some of the most noble of them, going along at the head of their troops in the full light of day, were suddenly blinded. Taken unawares by their enemies they were hemmed in on all sides, thrown down and slain. Few of their companions escaped – only those who had crossed themselves.

These marvels were performed by God's saint to avenge his wrongs.

## CHAPTER 68

### *The sign of the rainbow arc*

Now that our holy bishop had gone to the Lord, his abbots and their subjects were afraid their old enemies might take up the attack again.

'As long as our noble leader was alive,' they said to themselves, 'we endured numerous different trials at the hands of the kings and princes of Britain, all of which ended honourably for us, thanks to Wilfrid's wisdom and sanctity and the help of his friends. We must now believe, fully and without reservation, that we have an intercessor in Heaven raised up by the power of the Holy Cross to the level of his own beloved Saints Peter and Paul, to whose patronage he and his followers dedicated all their possessions. We must trust that, there in the sight of God, he guards and defends us unceasingly.'

Their trust was soon given warrant by a sign appearing in the heavens. On the anniversary of his death all our bishops and their abbots gathered together from north, south, east, and west to mark the solemn occasion. As they were keeping the evening vigil in the church where his remains rested, certain of the less watchful brethren standing outside saw a sign appear in the sky. They kept quiet about it till the next morning. When the rest heard about it they were deeply grieved and murmured to each other that it had been kept back from them because of their sins. Their honesty was soon rewarded. When the feast that ended the solemnities was over, the whole assembly went out of doors in the twilight to sing compline. Suddenly a wonderful white arc shone out before them in the heavens, encircling the entire monastery. Apart from the lack of colour it looked exactly like a rainbow. Starting from the gables of St Peter's basilica where Wilfrid's bones were laid to rest, it stretched towards the south, then made a wide sweep to the north round the right-hand side of the monastery before bending upwards into the south-eastern quarter of the morning sky. We worshipped and praised the Lord for this sign, the Lord who is wondrous in His saints, for we clearly saw that He was with us, building a wall of protection around his chosen vineyard. Our conviction was borne out in every event that rose to affright us. Regular monastic life continued to flourish under outstanding abbots in all kingdoms on both sides of the Humber and the brethren lived to see the enemies who massed against us pierced with their own barbs. As for us, to quote the Psalmist: 'In the name of our God we shall be exalted.'